GOD'S D

Also by Kathleen O'Sullivan

Light Out of Darkness

God's Delight

Opening Our Hearts to His love, Trust and Joy

Kathleen O'Sullivan SSL

Hodder & Stoughton
LONDON SYDNEY AUCKLAND

First published in Great Britain in 1996

10 9 8 7 6 5 4 3 2 1

British Library Cataloguing in Publication Data
A record for this book is available form the British Library

ISBN 0 340 62776 X

Typeset by Hewer Text Composition Services, Edinburgh
Printed and bound in Great Britain by
Cox & Wyman Ltd, Reading, Berks

Hodder and Stoughton Ltd
A Division of Hodder Headline PLC
338 Euston Road
London NW1 3BH

To Mary,
the Mother of Jesus and our Mother

CONTENTS

ACKNOWLEDGMENTS

To my St Louis Community, I wish to express my deep appreciation for their constant support and understanding.

To my friends and to all involved in 'Light Out of Darkness' prayer/life groups, I gratefully acknowledge their continually holding me and the writing of *God's Delight* before Almighty God in prayer.

In a special way, I wish to thank Dee Dannatt – not only for expert typing, artistic presentation, unfailing commitment, but also for sharing so generously with me her gift as a perceptive, sensitive reader.

I wish to express my deep appreciation to Carolyn Armitage, the editor, for her gentle, expert guidance; also to Hodder and Stoughton – and especially to Elspeth Taylor for affirmation and kind support.

Bibles Used

I used both the Jerusalem Bible and the Life Application Bible NIV, according as each suited my purpose.

FOREWORD

This is the third book in a human spiritual growth **trilogy**. It can, however, be profitably read on its own.

Book One, *A Way of Life*, dealt with getting to know our human selves and, through that gateway, our coming to know God. Later it was incorporated into Book Two, *Light Out of Darkness*.

The second book, *Light Out of Darkness*, explores more deeply the darker side of ourselves, its potential for deeper human and spiritual growth, and the transformation of darkness into light.

Book Three, *God's Delight*, centres on the Incarnation of Jesus Christ in His humanity and on the Incarnation today of the Risen Christ within us. **God's delight** is in each step of our salvation process, as we too (like Christ) are led by the Spirit. Our Christian life is intended to be a holy, wholesome and joy-filled adventure to the delight of the Trinity.

The mystery of Christ, incarnate in His own flesh two thousand years ago, continues today as the mystery of the Risen Lord, incarnate in our humanity. The call of our Christian life is to let the Risen Lord, the One who remains the Way, the Truth and the Life for us, live so deeply within us through the gift of His Spirit, that His power, His influence, His love affect and transform our thinking, our behaviour, our relationships with God and with one another.

God's delight is in His 'Chosen One', the Beloved Son in whom God the Father always sees and finds us, His beloved children. God's tenderness is such that He delights as Father in us, as we struggle to walk, as we fall but stagger perhaps grotesquely to our feet again, always loved and supported by Jesus, His ever-present 'First-born'. Our response of delight in God is true Christian joy and fullness of life, which is the grace-filled work of God's Holy Spirit.

Joy and rejoicing marked the birth of Jesus in Bethlehem. Joy marks the birth of Jesus, each day, in each event in you, in me, wherever God's children are. It happens unexpectedly in and through little, ordinary moments; but God's miracle of transforming love brings the ordinary and the infinite together, so that we, broken human beings, become more whole and more truly the image of God which is His divine intent for us.

INTRODUCTION

This book is essentially a message of hope! Hope for you, for me, for everyone today, tomorrow and all our tomorrows, despite all we hear and know about the wickedness of the world.

There is always room for hope when there is something that can be changed for the better. A great loss today is the absence of genuine love in too many places. This book is about the permanence of the greatest love-story that ever was and the invitation each of us receives to learn how to be transformed into a lover of God and a lover of His people! That takes courage! Are you willing? God partners us all the way through.

For a short time, I subscribed to the negative thinking about the evil of the world and the dreadful times in which we live. The effect on me was loss of verve, loss of enthusiasm and loss of love for others! Writing this book has transformed me and my thinking. I now see the world and times as 'different', requiring a different approach. Does that mean that I am 'indifferent' to the violence, the abuse, the greed, the corruption on a global scale? No, that cannot be tolerated, but my stance, my viewpoint has changed and that makes a difference that counts.

I allowed a corrupt world to deprive me of life. In this, I now recognise *the deadening effect of evil*. It manifested itself in my condemnation of everything and everyone 'out there', who could be blamed for the morass that surrounds us: the perpetrators of violence, of injustice, of abuse, of greed; dishonest politicians, abusers of the law, our hedonistic society, irresponsible parents, the Church; in fact, anyone, everyone – but what about myself?

In researching this theme, God's delight, and through a lot of prayerful reflection, I came to a few basic truths that restored my faith, my balance and my hope. I discovered how *real* in fact is God's delight with His people – especially in difficult times like the present.

His delight is in us, when we recognise and discover, by personal experience, that He truly is 'the Way forward', the 'Truth that sets free' and the 'Life' that reveals the falsity of the values of this world.

His delight is when we take personal responsibility to be fully alive, alert and challenging by living more deeply the life of faith, of hope, and of love which is our Christian heritage.

I rediscovered that God's love is always with us, supporting us, but that it is possible for any of us, even some of the time, to let our faith, our hope and our love grow faint if not actually cold. Out of that comes the awful truth that Almighty God is *not* loved. Every unloving act or thought of mine contributes to that reality. A truly awe-filling fact. And *that* is the tragedy of today: God is not loved, therefore God's people, that we all are, are unloved and unloving.

I rediscovered that there was a remedy for lack of love. St John of the Cross has it: 'Put love where there is no love and you will find love.' I found that in having compassion for my neighbour in his or her annoying little ways, I discovered the depths of my own 'unloving'. That startled me. In my becoming more understanding even of myself, Almighty God somehow became more central to my life and my efforts, and so He too became more loved!

My deep conviction is that the meaning of the healing power of Christ's Incarnation has more or less been lost today. It has been weakening for decades or more. Even Christmas cards with a message that recalls the birth of Christ can be difficult to find.

Christ's Incarnation is the *the saving action* of a God who loves His people passionately. It is not limited to His human experience in Nazareth nor even to the death on Calvary. The Risen Christ continues the mystery of the Incarnation by living within us in the power of the Spirit – if we are open to receive Him. The total mystery of the Incarnation affects our salvation and our growth in Christ. It is thus that we are energised to respond and to co-operate in love. Our faith, our hope and our love will grow when we allow the mystery of the Incarnation to transform our lives.

This is the answer to the problem of today. We tend to forget Christ – thus colluding with His enemies; we tend to rely on ourselves too much – thus condemning ourselves to mediocrity. Christ is our Saviour. Let us confess Him and worship Him. Let us entrust ourselves to Him in **faith**, in **hope** and in **love**!

A JOURNEY OF LOVE

1

GOD'S DELIGHT

The very title, 'God's Delight', raises my heart as I say it and when I rest in it, I find a smile on my face. When I name the title to others, I recognise the same response! Some verbalise it in various ways: 'I like that. It does something for me'; or 'That is beautiful. Can I really be a delight to God? How truly wonderful'; 'If that is true, it almost seems too good to be true, yet somehow I feel that maybe it is, maybe this is the *hope* that I'm longing for.'

My friends, **it is true**. Scripture will prove it to us. Our own experience will confirm this truth for us. The experience of others, of God's people the Body of Christ, is a tremendous testimony as we shall see. **God delights in us, His beloved people!**

God's delight is essentially rooted in Jesus Christ, His well-beloved Son, our Saviour.

God's delight therefore is essentially bound up with everything, with every detail that has to do with our experience of salvation.

God's delight therefore is intimately involved with you and me, who so badly need salvation.

This is surely the Good News!

That we can delight Almighty God at every moment

of our lives – given right attitudes – can be quite a shock for us who do not know the God of love and have been nurtured for too long on a God of fear.

I already hear some of you clamouring: 'But, but . . .'

Yes, we are sinners. That is a good place to begin, but how we begin is an important factor.

> Do not be afraid, for I have redeemed you;
> I have called you by your name, you are mine.
> Should you pass through the sea, I will be with you;
> or through rivers, they will not swallow you up.
> Should you walk through fire, you will not be scorched
> and the flames will not burn you.
> For I am Yahweh, your God,
> the Holy One of Israel, your Saviour. (Isa. 43:1–3)

Yes, let us look the truth about ourselves in the face, and claim it: we are sinners. There is no one exempt from that reality, otherwise we make God out to be a liar (1 John 5:10) but, likewise, there is nobody to whom salvation is not offered.

In all this question of our sinfulness, let us keep the focus on God, on His unchanging love, on the potential that lies within each of us of being a delight to God when we believe in Him, trust Him, and turn to Him with the heart of a child. Miracles will begin to happen!

Another of the 'but, buts' that I hear from you is: 'How can I possibly delight God? *I don't do anything great for Him.'*

What kind of a God do we worship? Where did we get this idea of having to be wonder-persons, superman or woman?! I hear God talking in scripture about being little and ordinary and loving and having a care for one another. The Son of God emptied Himself and became a dweller in a backwater. In this very experience of a deceptive 'but' that you long to articulate, you and I can straight away delight God without any more ado. How?

Let's keep before our minds and hearts that God's delight flows from every detail connected with our salvation. Face deception in the smallest things, liberate the truth and you have delighted God in coming into true salvation!

We are dependent on God for everything. He is lavish with His response to our needs, but we must acknowledge that all gifts are from God, His messages of love. We don't want to become thieves, claiming as ours what is God's. Pride urges us to do this. Pride deceives us into thinking that God needs us to do great things for Him! It is so absurd when we let the truth flow: Almighty God can raise up legions of angels to do His bidding, to do all the great things that may be needed (or that we like to fantasise are needed). This allows us in imagination to bask in reflected glory; alas, it also misdirects our energy from the one and only thing God truly wants from us, and which we alone can give Him, namely the love of our heart! We use everything to escape giving our heart, because as sinners, we love ourselves more than we love God or other people.

One other basic attitude will open the way for us to delight God from the very start. It is to recognise that even in the giving of our heart to God, **we cannot do anything of ourselves.** Without the help of God, we cannot say: 'Abba, Father!' Without the power and love of God, we cannot open our hearts and be faithful. God is the source of all the good in our lives. Once we accept that, with joy and gladness, we have a different vision; we are sharing in the true vision of Almighty God. By living that, by trustfully accepting with Jesus that God is our Father, we begin to delight in our potential for delighting Him. We may, as His beloved child, begin by saying to Him: 'Help me give You my whole heart.' We may eventually end by saying: 'My beloved God, give me Your own love to love You with; take my heart and give me Yours, so that You can do what You like in me and through me.'

My friends, don't believe me, that would be foolish indeed. Beg for humility and be willing to take God's pace. Then try out *for yourself* some of the above. Savour it; rest in God. Delight in Him and He will delight in you! Thus you learn *from your own experience*. You are discerning, in the power of the Spirit, alive and working within you, how Almighty God is teaching you. It raises our spiritual adrenaline to keep alight in our hearts those powerful words of scripture from both Isaiah and St John:

> All your sons will be taught by the Lord
> and great will be your children's peace.
>
> (Isa. 54:13)

and St John:

> 'They will be taught by God. Everyone who listens to the Father and learns from Him comes to me,' says Jesus. (John 6:45)

Yes, we are sinners, but God keeps calling us out of darkness into light, into His presence, into the experience of salvation, which has ever new depths to be explored.

GOD'S DELIGHT

We gradually begin to discover that we have only this present moment, this hour of salvation, in which to delight God, by whatever we desire, do, think or try to become. St Paul quotes Isaiah:

> In the time of my favour I heard you
> and in the day of salvation I helped you.

and then stresses the *urgency* of the time:

> I tell you, now is the time of God's favour, now is the day of salvation. (2 Cor. 6:2)

How do we use the gift of this 'now', this present moment, so as to delight our God? It is so simple. Become aware of your own natural delight, recognise it as a gift of God calling you to remember that your delight is the overflow of God's own delight! All delight, like all other good things, comes from above, from the heart of our God. You can use your experience of delight so as to enter more deeply into the source of all delight, the fullness of God. Take, for example, an experience of sheer natural beauty, or the song of a bird breaking the utter stillness around, or the sight of mischievous laughter on the face of an innocent child. Take whatever it is that moves you. That movement is the Spirit of God alight within you, calling for a sharing of delight! Whatever seems right for you to do at that moment, do it. Follow your deepest instinct. You may feel tears prickling your eyes, which can happen when the inner joy is almost too close, or you may just rest, immovable in Presence, wrapped around by the Invisible, *still, reverent, grateful*; or you may, momentarily, seem to be taken out of yourself with the unexpectedness of the utter simplicity and joy of just *being*. Whatever your experience of delight may be, stay with it; savour it; as you gently return to the workaday world, give thanks, heartfelt thanks for the moment of bliss.

It is helpful to recall the line of the psalmist: 'Delight yourself in the Lord and he will give you the desires of your heart' (Ps. 37:4). This verse from scripture seems to me to catch a deep truth about the *quality* of delight. Delight has a transparent spontaneous quality, hasn't it? There is a childlike glow about the very word and the effect of a smile breaking on one's face. 'Delight' is not static, nor studied; there is nothing coy nor falsely grown-up about 'delight'. It has movement, it is alive, the Spirit of God is in it. It is the essential mark of a child of God!

Pause for a moment, if you feel drawn, and think of the child Jesus messing around the carpenter's shop, discovering the wonder of wood shavings, the feel of them against his cheek, the novel smell of them and maybe the temptation to lick them and try them out! There you have God's delight, looking at His Son, the Word made flesh. Or look at the ninety-year-old granny, as I did, when she managed to hide a floury, forbidden boiled potato up her big sleeve. Her delight lay in outwitting her loving minders; but her greatest delight was when the potato rolled out of her sleeve to the floor and she and her grandchild shared mutual disgrace!

Again, God's delight is 'to be with his children'. Why don't we delight more in God and His gifts and so share delight with Him?! God is a great teacher and He longs to have the opportunity in the present moment, the present experience, no matter what it is, to let you see how much He delights in your efforts. It doesn't really matter whether you are led to begin with your own experience of delight or with seeking to recognise God's delight in all forms of His creation, all becomes eventually, in the power of the Spirit, a song of great beauty, a song of love.

At this stage, someone may want to rebel and say: 'So, I must be always good, doing what pleases God, doing all perfectly before He can delight in me. Is that it?' No, that isn't it, though if you keep seeking God's delight, you will certainly discover your own and you will be happy and content. But let us look briefly at another kind of experience, where God delights in us, weak and rebellious children. Take, for example, yourself as you are now, if you are the one who wants to rebel. God will always delight in you as long as you keep hanging in there! Your struggle to find Him touches Him deeply and He delights in you. He is not a sadist and is not delighting in pain, but we all have our dark and difficult times and only God can draw good out of those black experiences. God never gives up on us; as long as we do not deliberately and continuously reject Him and stubbornly refuse to let the slightest movement touch us, He is holding on to us more than we can ever long to hold on to Him and He delights to be able to help us at such times. Only God can search out with infinite generosity and magnanimity the extenuating circumstances that give Him a loophole to reach us a helping hand. Even when we seem to say 'NO, I want to have nothing to do with You', our God is still gently sifting our rubble to find just a glimmer of desire within us. On this He builds and His delight is great at the slightest clutching of our hand in His, even though it may surely come from the fear of drowning and being lost. We will never grasp just how precious we are to God and how He will suffer anything so as to bring us safely home. Let us never forget that **God's delight is intertwined with anything at all that deals with our salvation!**

On this matter of salvation, however, God wants us to be *real and genuine*. He will never let us harm ourselves or lessen the depth of salvation which is open to us by letting us attempt to manipulate Him. God is Truth, so deception, make-believe, dishonesty or game-playing will not be accepted as coinage for salvation. It is not sacrifices or oblations that God is seeking, but 'an open and contrite heart'. God seeks in every way to open us to a deeper faith in Him, deeper hope and trust and above all deeper love. If we want to be open with God, then we begin with our brothers and sisters. If we are genuine, meaning what we say and do with our neighbour, then we will do the same with God. We are delighting God when we become free to accept how He is drawing us into closer love relationship with Himself. His delight increases accordingly as we open up to His love for us and give Him space and time to talk to us and to touch our hearts. Yes, we delight God greatly when we persevere even though it is difficult, when we hope against hope, when we believe though we seem so dry and all seems fruitless. We are the work of His hands, the fruit of His love and He will never desert us. We will rather be able to say: 'He brought me out into a spacious place; he rescued me because he delighted in me' (Ps. 18:19).

Let us rejoice therefore; let us be glad, and indeed His delight will be great. The wonder of it all – that Almighty God can use even me, to let His delight overflow and bring joy to His beloved people.

Through the years, it has helped me greatly whenever I read something that spoke to me, to pause and to note what exactly made an impression on me. Out of all that, I learnt to be still before God and let the Spirit bring to my awareness the most important point in that reading for me. I would hold that point in my awareness, letting God take care of it for me. I knew that in His own way, He would teach me whatever was important for me to learn.

He will do the work within us, provided that our hearts and desires are rooted in Him. It's amazing how close God comes to one when we trust Him like that: 'Like a weaned child on its mother's breast' (Ps. 131: 2).

A Chance to Reflect

(if you desire)

- *I find it full of hope that God can be delighted through something I may do!*
- *In this present moment, this 'Now', I can delight God in many ways: by whispering my love to Him; by doing a kind, loving thing for another person; by delighting in somebody's good fortune and sharing that delight with God!*
- *God is greatly delighted when I struggle against my weaknesses – then we are partners in working out my salvation.*
- *God loves little gestures of love. He receives them with joy and delight; He showers my day with little gifts – a smile from someone, a helping hand . . . all are His messengers of love, saying: 'I delight in you.'*

A Chance to Pray

(in simple words, perhaps something like the following – or to pray by being silent but alert to His presence)

Thank you, Lord God, for teaching me during that silent time together! Help me to put Your teaching into practice in my daily life. Above all, dear Lord, help me to love You, to delight in You. I believe that You delight in me, this moment, as we spend time together loving one another.

Stay with me, Lord, and with everyone I meet this day. Let Your love and Your delight flow through me to Your beloved people.

2

LOVE AND DELIGHT

It is time now to look more deeply at this gift of love which has priority in the whole *salvation experience*. Through the love of the Godhead, we have been redeemed. Through the love of our Saviour, Jesus Christ, we have been given new life and given new power through sharing the Spirit of Love. The mandate to love one another as God has loved us marks the path before us very clearly.

Yet even among Christians – and perhaps we ought to say, *especially* among Christians (since we Christians cannot plead ignorance) – we have been sadly remiss. Jesus taught us about the primacy of love. The gift of the Holy Spirit keeps reminding us about all He taught us, as He promised would happen, and yet we have, in monstrous fashion, abused the gift of love.

We have spoken much about delight and the question may be asked whether delight and love are the same experience. The essence of God, His very nature, is love. Various manifestations of this essential nature of God are revealed to us, as, for example, His mercy, compassion, justice, magnanimity or generosity, joy and delight. But love is the *root*, the source of all else, just as God Himself is the Source of all that is good. Delight and gladness and rejoicing seem to be akin, but love, properly understood, embraces all else.

Love is creative, and wherever the Spirit of Love is operating, the result will be fruitful and joyful creativity. Because love is so misunderstood today, I want to try to express it in a different way, so that creative spirits may catch on and be inflamed by God's Spirit of Love. Then we can 'fan into a flame the gift [of love] that God has given us . . . we have been trusted to look after something precious; [we must] guard it with the help of the Holy Spirit who lives in us' (2 Tim. 1:6, 14). In the following verses, there is a mingling of love and delight, which seem to merge at times yet leave the supremacy to love! Let God's love grasp you and hold you gently, as you read. Rest in that love. Let go what does not, as yet, speak to you:

God is Love.
Love is the essence of God.
'Delight' is a manifestation of God's Unchanging Love.

Love is exciting.
Love is creativity in its fullness;
Love is newness of life in its every facet.

Love challenges to live deeply, daringly,
beyond known frontiers.

God's delight is to be Himself,
free to pour out His Love without limit;
free to recreate always,
us and His creation.

LOVE AND DELIGHT

God's love delights in the human response,
from the cavern of love within,
a response totally beyond our human limitations,
within His essence, startling us;
God's love, delighting,
drawing life from within us,
between us,
between us and the Godhead,
abounding with joy in being Saviour
to our nothingness,
holding our finite fragility
'in sinu patris' – the Father's bosom,
in the Son, 'nearest to the Father's heart';
aflame in the love of the Spirit,
setting us alight!

Delight surges within the Trinity
enriching, saving our lost humanity.

Delight in the Chosen One, the Son,
in Whom the Father so delights.
Delight in His emptying of divine trappings
Breaking frontiers to our human poverty
becoming flesh to be like us;
easing the unstinted flow
of Trinitarian love.

Conceived by Love itself
in the womb of the humble handmaid,
– Love's resting-place.
Love at home
where God is all
where self is naught

GOD'S DELIGHT

where Love delights
to rejoice.

Obedience – the heart seeking,
the ear listening,
the whole being
open to wait,
to watch for the One who comes,
open to surrender,
to die,
so that God-Life be in a womb . . .
. . . and the Word made flesh
dwelt among us.

Delight of God –
the Word made flesh
was seen
was touched
was loved by
other humans;

Tiny fingers
doing human things
little things,
teaching
you and me
to read, to learn, to follow
His way, His true way
of giving life,
a way of love,
a story of love
that costs all,
leading to ecstasy!

LOVE AND DELIGHT

Why hesitate?
Why plod the dull path?
Why starve on a crumb,
rejecting a banquet?
Why burrow in a warren
when soaring mountains challenge a climb?
Why whisper
when God's glory can be proclaimed from housetops?
Why be less than human
when He has made us little less than gods?

Do we choose to stay in the cold
while everlasting arms reach
to hold us in close embrace?
Why let a neighbour die
when our love-lifting
places him in protective arms?

Why choose to walk
when we're offered the magic
of eagles' wings?
Are we not His children
hearing unceasingly
His croon of love
'My delight is to be with you'?
Listen and learn:
'My foolish children,
slow to believe
that I am your God
who made you
who loves you tenderly
you, My people.'

GOD'S DELIGHT

'Love transforms
makes beautiful
makes whole,
Come and be loved.
Come! come close, come and rest on My waiting heart.
Come, let Me teach you, my children.
Let Me love you
into your becoming love;
Come, you are precious
all are precious.
Rest in Me
filled with My Spirit,
others will see
will draw close
as sisters and brothers,
and love –
our love –
will bring forth
new life, new hope,
new heaven on earth.
Let joy, let delight
burst forth!'

A Chance to Reflect

(if you desire)

- *Lord, I look forward to these little silences. They help me meet You, listen to You, learn how You are teaching me to deepen our love-relationship. I begin to value that more each time. It's the way a human relationship develops and now You teach me that is the way You and I also grow closer! Thank You, God.*
- *Help me to discover creativity all around me, within myself, within others, in Your beautiful world. Help me discover the gifts of creativity that you have put within me, to delight in and with You when we develop those gifts together!*
- *Let me be courageous and believe in the Truth that the Blessed Trinity lives within me. Let that thought awaken in me the great desire – and delight – in being with You, in working with You, in listening to You, in seeking You in myriad places and when I find You, let me praise and glorify and thank You.*
- *Help me to discover that 'obedience' is a love-word, not a series of do's and don'ts. The do's and don'ts can be a meeting place where my growing love for You gives a multi-coloured hue to the obedience, the hue of delight and love.*
- *Help me to treasure the gift of Jesus when He became human for love of me. Let me be creative and sing love-songs to Him, when I'm in the car, or walking, or in the bath. It can all be in silence, and that can include happy laughter!*

A Chance to Pray

(as you feel drawn – the following are but suggestions)

Lord, You are truly wonderful and full of surprises. Thank You. Let me learn to become increasingly more still, so that my listening to You is not disturbed by unnecessary noise, fidgeting or distractions. Fill me and the whole world with Your Spirit, so that You are present and acting powerfully everywhere. Thank You, Lord, be praised and glorified and delighted with Your children!

Lord, please sharpen my inner hearing, so that I can actually 'hear' silence, and learn to understand its message. For this great gift, I thank you, Lord.

I also ask it for my neighbour, who is highly strung. She has suffered much and would benefit greatly from learning to relax in Your silence and stillness. You are a great Teacher, Lord, teach my friend and also all other people who have nobody to help them.

If we listened better to one another, Lord, there would be less violence in the world, because listening to one another is the first step to listening to you, isn't it, Lord?

3

SCRIPTURE AND GOD'S DELIGHT

For those who may still be questioning if it is really true that our God, whom we have offended so often, so grievously and so selfishly, can really delight in us His wayward children, we turn to scripture for the word of truth that will convince and set us free!

First, however, there are some things about scripture that I long to share with you, even though you may already know them all. Since I am in no way an exegete, I hope that my own personal experience will have something to say to ordinary people like myself.

Scripture – the word of God Himself! When I stood before the Rock of Abraham a short time ago in God's own land, the Holy Land, I was rooted in scripture. I was keenly aware of two rocks in Jerusalem, that dearly loved city of God: Abraham's rock in the Dome of the Rock and the Rock of the Agony of our beloved Jesus, in Gethsemane, in the Church of All Nations.

Two rocks; one God; yet nations divided. That reality became for me a sea of pain. The fact remains, however, that even the deepest of noble emotions remains barren unless it gives rise to *healing action*. I know that embedded in my own daily life lies a responsibility to discover anything disruptive – no matter how slight – in my daily relations with brothers and sisters. That is a beginning, but it is not enough. To eschew, to get rid of the evil, the darkness of a broken brother-sisterhood in my life is the essential 'rock' on which I must reconstruct. That must be claimed, owned and courageously faced. In *my* daily life – as in the Incarnation of the Word made flesh – the human and the divine must become one. If I sincerely desire this wholeness and let God help me, it will be done, as Isaiah tells us:

> . . . my word that goes out from my mouth
> will not return to me empty,
> but will accomplish what I desire
> and achieve the purpose for which I sent it.
> You will go out in joy
> and be led forth in peace. (Isa. 55:11–12)

So, in our 'little lives', the word of God will achieve God's purpose in us, provided that we too, like our forebears, Abraham and Jesus Christ, are the children of God who are *obedient* to the call of love. We need to face the truth of our Christian lives: we are continuously faced with choices; the 'rock' of my life can become a saving rock, not only for myself but, in the mercy of God, a rock of salvation for another, when we **listen, learn, and are taught by God to obey in love**, or – awesome choice – it can remain a rock that obstructs the flow of saving life.

> But if your heart turns away and you are not obedient . . . I declare to you this day that you will certainly be

> destroyed . . . I have set before you life and death . . . choose life, so that you and your children may live and that you may love the Lord, your God, listen to his voice and hold fast to him. For the Lord is your life . . . (Deut. 30:17–18)

As I have tried in the past to listen more humbly to the word of God and to be 'taught by God', as both Isaiah and St John admonish us (Isa. 54:13; John 6:45), I discover that I have been taught some truths which have helped me. These I wish to share with you in the hope that someone else may find them useful.

A word, a phrase, a concept in scripture may move us. In my young days, I used to get excited about this and was led by God to seek how I could *enflesh* such a word into my daily life. Two such lines became my life-line when I first entered religious life in 1938. Little did I know that in my receiving these verses from God and in trying to enflesh them in ordinary actions, like washing dishes, polishing floors, eating, turning the other cheek in trivialities, that God was already training me to write *A Way of Life* and *Light Out of Darkness* some fifty years later![1] God has a plan for each of us and every beginning is small. Two verses of scripture changed my life. God does wonderful things with very little. The work is His; the power is His; the love is His. The response is ours supported by His Spirit.

The verses of scripture which changed my life were: 'Willingly do I rejoice in my weaknesses, so that the strength of Christ may be in me' (2 Cor. 12:10); and 'I live now not I but Christ lives in me' (Gal. 2:20). In those far-off days, we had not the luxury of formal spiritual direction, as happens today, but I do not regret it. Without it, I had to develop the habit of bringing all to Jesus in the Blessed Sacrament. I didn't know that through these two verses from scripture – one dealing with my weaknesses and my pains, the other dealing with the strength to cope with any cross or 'rock' in life – that I was receiving down-to-earth teaching from Jesus Himself. I knew nothing then about discernment. I know now that when I had been helped, psychologically, by pouring out all my problems to Him, I was better able to *listen* to God; I learnt to wait!

There is much I want to say about 'waiting' on God's word in scripture. I sat with Him, resting, because I had nowhere else to go! When I became still and at peace, I used to look at the 'problem' again. It was less black. And as I listened, I then began to look at what seemed right for me to do; I discovered that peace remained as long as my choice to let go, to trust God, remained paramount. Somehow, I came to learn that God was *for* me, as scripture says: 'If God is for us, who can be against us?' (Rom. 8:31); but more important still, I also discovered that when I acted *against my weakness* – for example, by turning the other cheek, or by admitting I was prone to judge rashly and needed to let the Spirit of God 'gentle' my mode of thinking – joy surged through my being. The experience of that particular kind of joy used to lure me into action. It certainly was a most welcome push!

Letting ourselves be 'taught by God' is a very powerful gift. Its validity is rooted in scripture: 'By their fruits you will know them' (Matt. 7:16). The fruits can be clearly recognised by oneself. When my anger abates, or my self-centred concern with my hurts or my so-called rights lessens and diminishes, leaving me space to breathe more freely, I know God is present and is teaching me. When I begin to be more concerned about the rights of others, more in touch with how Jesus is seeing all this, I know that God has released His healing Spirit upon my spirit and – even momentarily – we are one. Each time, however, I must be willing to recognise and claim my weakness; I must be ready to change my warp, then God's strength is there to help me. **Thus I learn to live, by letting Christ live in me**. There is a lifetime's work there. God gives us all the time we need.

As my life in Christ seemed to develop a little more, and especially in latter years, I've tended to surrender the initial enthusiastic excitement which I mentioned, when I would be struck by a word and immediately begin to see how to live it out that day. Life has taught me several things: the importance of 'waiting on God's time' to reveal the deeper truth of His word. Lately, I have discovered that for some words of God, it has taken me twenty-five years, for another, fifty years, for the real truth of one particular word to percolate and blossom. This does not mean that those words of God went fallow or were not used by Him in the intervening years. I think the true meaning is that it required the transforming action of God's Spirit on me during those intervening years to ready me, to mature me, to help me hear and understand the depth of His initial word.

In the beginning, this waiting can be very painful! We are so used to taking control and running things our way, that, at times, there may be a strong temptation to get on with it, to work for God rather than let God lead and teach one through patient waiting on His will. Waiting may gradually become less painful but it is never truly an easy experience!

It is, however, a most rewarding one. I find the ultimate dawning of light, the awareness of His touch and His guidance quite wonderful and exhilarating. It recalls the scriptural quotation on how a woman in labour forgets the pain when she holds her child in her arms. In spiritual terms, it is like a post-graduate course which keeps the spirit alight and alive; it energises and stimulates creativity; but it also – somehow – calms and makes still, in a way that is new, at least to my nature. This is not a new *experience*; rather it is a richer quality of a former touch, that now opens up a vista of sheer beauty; it also deepens the understanding of God's love. That deeper unfolding of God's presence can make one tremble as does the unknown, yet it fills with a trust which, at least momentarily, is like strong, impregnable **faith**; it instils **hope** which looks forward without fear, nestling like a snowdrop on a bank of green leaves, sure harbinger of the increasing **love** that binds all together.

The intervening years have also taught me that while the word of scripture has a special unction, yet our God speaks, in a million other ways, without *words* always being necessary. What a pity if God speaks and His words are not allowed to be life-giving. When God 'spoke', you and I came into being! **We are God's spoken word**; He made us in the hope that one of the ways in which He could be with us was when we would become His sounding-board for our brothers and sisters. Alas, how many voices of unborn brothers and sisters are stifled in the womb, never permitted to let their little beings reverberate with God's voice of love within them! St Paul tells us also that we are the *'letters of Christ'*, that people should be able to read His presence in our hearts on meeting us:

SCRIPTURE AND GOD'S DELIGHT

> It is plain that you are a letter from Christ . . . written with the Spirit of the loving God, not on stone tablets but on the tablets of your living hearts.
>
> (2 Cor. 3:3)

The letters which we actually write could also well be a chosen vehicle wherein God's voice of compassion, of gentleness, of support, of love is expressed, or is He perhaps asking, at times, for a voice of challenge to be heard, expressed in a gentle tone to help us become more honest, more real?

However many are God's ways of speaking, the voice that has resounded most for me in latter years is that of the neighbour, the *Body of Christ*. Through this voice, I have experienced many gifts: support; direction, at times in ways I would rather not go; rejection; misunderstanding; hurt; affirmation; confirmation; tenderness; a call to ministry; a clearer recognition of His voice in the sharing of a vision that clarifies my own . . . And always necessary is the same approach as marks the 'hearing' of scripture – to be humble, alert, listening, discerning the movements within oneself, to be open, waiting, focusing on the voice, discerning, confirming decisions by their fruits, *always* looking for the sign of the Spirit of God whose mark is clear – peace, joy, love, a dying to self that others may live.

It may now be easier for us to hear more clearly that voice in scripture which can touch our depths, can affect our lives as no other power on earth can, revealing God's delight.

Like healthy children who spontaneously seek first the sweetest and most delectable of proffered goodies, having none of the gastronomic anxieties of later years, we too will taste scripture, be nourished and rejoice. Let us remember that God's delight can be expressed in the word 'delight', or too in words like 'rejoice' and 'gladness of heart' or in *descriptions* of joy and delight. My hope is that hereafter we will be on the alert to rejoice with the Lord whenever possible, and to discover new delights in our reading of scripture.

We will start with a good rousing example from Zephaniah:

> Shout for joy, daughter of Zion,
> Israel, shout aloud.
> Rejoice, exult with all your heart,
> O daughter of Jerusalem!
> The Lord has taken away your punishment,
> he has turned back your enemy.
> The Lord, the King of Israel, is with you;
> never again will you fear any harm.
> On that day, they will say to Jerusalem,
> Do not fear, O Zion;
> do not let your hands hang limp.
> The Lord your God is with you,
> he is mighty to save.
> **He will take great delight in you,**
> he will quiet you with his love,
> he will *rejoice* over you with singing.
>
> (Zeph. 3:14–17) (emphasis mine)

Each of us has to listen and be obedient to God's voice and the guidance of the Spirit in our own regard. Nevertheless, we are also used by God to help one another. A dear friend, in writing to me one day, enclosed the above quote from Zephaniah. It set me alight and as I copied it just now, there was a recurrence of the same joy, gladness and glowing presence. I stopped, so as to delight the Lord by bringing before Him all who needed to experience gladness today. I find it seems to delight God greatly when we *share with others* the gifts He gives ourselves. I find that coming closer to God is frequently done in such little moments, little drawings by the Spirit, which refresh, exhilarate, enlighten, and remind us of our own smallness and our dependence on one another. When God gives us a task to do for Him – like writing this book – He gives all the nourishment we need, including some necessary fasting periods when one wonders where He has gone to! He does not seem to overwhelm us, however, so that we can't proceed, at least not little ones like me. In all things He is gentle, compassionate and understanding.

The word 'smallness' reminds me of another friend whose Christmas card held me 'in God' for a long time. Again, it teaches me how God speaks to us in various ways through one another. The quote on the card that moved me was from Hilaire Belloc. Underneath the tiny form of the child in the crib was printed:

He was so small
you could not see
His large intent
of courtesy.

I found it a touching and near-perfect description of the amazing mystery of the Incarnation.

To return to the quote from Zephaniah, he says that the Lord Himself will disperse Israel's enemies (therefore ours too) and come to live among His people. He will give gladness. We sin when we pursue happiness by cutting ourselves off from fellowship with God. As Zephaniah points out, gladness results when we allow God to be with us, teaching us. But always, from us must come a **personal response of faithful obedience**. Thus, we liberate our God to rejoice over us with singing.

I find that it isn't sufficient to read this, or to know it 'in our heads'. We need to reflect on it with the help of God's Spirit of Love, so that we can apply what we learn to our daily lives and thus discover what must change so that we release God's delight!

To give emphasis to that point, let us look at this quote from Malachi (3:7, 8). Israel had been disobedient, as we sinners are, and God had to call out to them, *teaching them*. His cry resounded:

> 'Return to me and I will return to you' says Yahweh Sabaoth.
> But you ask, 'How are we to return?'
> 'Will a man rob God? Yet you rob me.'

This was for the Israelites a matter of paying tithes and the people refused, fearing to lose what they had worked so hard to get. We too need to remember the teaching of Jesus that applies to our daily lives and take care to do what pleases God:

> Do not judge and you will not be judged.
> Do not condemn and you will not be condemned.
> Forgive and you will be forgiven.
> Give and it will be given to you.
> A good measure, pressed down, shaken together and running over will be poured into your lap.

> For with the measure you use, it will be measured to
> you. (Luke 6:37–38)

The lesson is simple: if we wish to experience the delight of our God, we must delight in him and delight to fulfil His commands (Ps. 40:8).

Here Isaiah is being persuasive, so that delight follows our listening and obeying:

> Seek Yahweh while he is still to be found,
> call to him while he is still near . . .
> . . . turn back to Yahweh who will take pity,
> to our God who is rich in forgiving;
> for my thoughts are not your thoughts,
> my ways not your ways – it is Yahweh who
> speaks. (Isa. 55:6–8)

And Jeremiah urges us likewise, in a letter to the captive exiles in Babylon:

> I know the plans I have for you, plans to prosper you, not to harm you, plans to give you hope and a future. Then you will come and pray to me and I will listen to you. You will seek me and find me when you seek me with all your heart. I will be found by you and will bring you back from captivity.
> (Jer. 29:11–14)

That passage from Jeremiah reminds us perhaps of the father in the parable of the Prodigal Son (Luke 15:11–31). Who is seeking the more urgently in the passage from Jeremiah, the captive exiles or their God? Whose delight is held in check? Who is the captive? Whose love is more selfless?

The psalmist in Psalm 37 uses the same persuasive tactics:

> Delight yourself in the Lord
> and he will give you the desires of your heart.
> (Ps. 37:4)

At other times, the psalmist is more direct:

> For the Lord takes delight in his people
> He crowns the **humble** with salvation. (Ps. 149:4)

and again:

> The Lord delights in those
> who put their **hope** in His unfailing love.
> (Ps. 147:11) (emphasis mine)

The psalms are rich in praise and thanksgiving. These bring us into close contact with the truth of where we ourselves are with regard to true worship of God. If we are genuinely seeking God – no matter how we stumble – then we are desiring God with all our hearts and this is a delight to God Himself.

In our leisure times, we can grow in discovering God's delight which we can release by adding to our own discoveries in the psalms. Some starting points might be Psalms 136, 135, 138; special mention, I think, must be made of Psalm 139 where God, through the psalmist, exults in knowing us so intimately, the One 'who knit me in my mother's womb'! The God who loves me is everywhere. I can never be lost to His Spirit, never far from the Presence of the One who protects, loves, guides and knows me through and through. Even if at times I feel worthless, God will never forsake me. In the words of Isaiah, if a mother should neglect her child, God will never do so:

> Yet even if these forget
> I will never forget you.
> See I have engraved you on the palms of my
> hands. (Isa. 49:15)

When we ponder and reflect on this passage and are led by the Spirit, we will doubtless want to cry out exultantly with Isaiah who has said:

> Shout for joy, O heavens,
> rejoice, O earth;
> burst into song, O mountains!
> For the Lord comforts his people
> and will have compassion on his afflicted ones.
> (Isa. 49:13)

Isaiah is one of my favourite prophets on account of the strengthening message of comfort and delight which he gives us, and do we not need this kind of spiritual injection at times?! Chapter 12 in Isaiah is a hymn of praise. Isaiah's message of hope looks forward to the coming of the Messiah. Here is a graphic description of the people's joy when the Messiah comes to rule over the earth. We, too, can rejoice at the renewed hope of Christ the Messiah entering more deeply into our lives. Surely a cause of delight. We can pour out our thanks, our gratitude, our praise. We can spread the Good News and manifest our own delight and desire for closeness with Jesus Christ.

> Surely God is my salvation:
> I will trust and not be afraid.
> The Lord, the Lord, is my strength and my song;
> he has become my salvation.
> With joy you will draw water
> from the wells of salvation . . .
> Give thanks to the Lord, call on his name;
> make known among the nations what he has done,
> and proclaim that his name is exalted.
> Sing to the Lord, for he has done glorious things;
> let this be known to all the world.
> Shout aloud and sing for joy, people of Zion,
> for great is the Holy One of Israel among you.
> (Isa. 12:2–6)

From chapter 58 in Isaiah to the end, there are many excerpts revealing the joy and therefore the **delight** of God.

> Arise, shine, for your light has come,
> and the glory of the Lord rises upon you . . .
> Lift up your eyes and look about you:
> All assemble and come to you . . .
> Then you will look and be radiant,
> your heart will throb and swell with joy . . .
> I will make you the everlasting pride and the joy of all generations . . .
> Then you will know that I, the Lord, am your Saviour,

your Redeemer, the Mighty One of Jacob.
(Isa. 60:1, 4, 5, 15, 16)

We may feel drawn to pause and to reflect how fortunate we Christians are, who believe that the Messiah has come and that the fulfilment of God's promises is in this present time. In chapter 61, we can read the verses – quoted later by Christ in the synagogue in Nazareth – and know for ourselves the truth of the words spoken by Christ: 'Today this scripture is fulfilled in your hearing' (Luke 4:21).

The Spirit of the Lord God is upon me,
because the Lord has anointed me
to bring good tidings to the afflicted;
He has sent me to bind up the broken-hearted,
to proclaim liberty to the captives . . . (Isa. 61:1)

Of all these chapters from Isaiah, my favourite is chapter 62; we need to remember that we are *the new Jerusalem,* that we will be called by a new name, a name that the Lord Himself will bestow. That was a memorable and helpful experience for me during a thirty-day retreat and so this chapter speaks clearly to me. Let us look at some verses, and see how one can be brought into the light out of darkness; one can rejoice in the gift of joy given by the compassionate Lord:

You will be a crown of splendour in the Lord's hand,
a royal diadem in the hand of your God.
No longer will they call you Deserted
or name your land Desolate.
But you will be called 'My Delight'

and your land 'the Wedded';
for Yahweh takes delight in you
and your land will have its wedding.
Like a young man marrying a virgin,
so will the one who built you wed you,
and as the bridegroom rejoices in his bride,
so will your God rejoice in you. (Isa. 62:3–5)

In chapter 65, Isaiah speaks of 'new heavens and a new earth'. These are eternal and in them safety, peace and plenty will be available.

Be glad and rejoice for ever
in what I will create
for I will create Jerusalem to be a delight
and its people a joy.
I will rejoice over Jerusalem
and take delight in my people. (Isa. 65:18–19)

At this stage, some may feel crowded by *quotes* and long perhaps to pause, to spend time allowing the Lord just to be present. Then follow that lead. If instead we are called to a word of healing, of transformation, of recognition, that indeed my ways and thoughts differ greatly from the Lord's, then receive that gift with gladness and rest there. We delight our God by sitting humbly at His feet, letting Him do as He will with us.

In chapter 66, He Himself says:

This is the one I esteem
he who is humble and contrite in spirit
and trembles at my word. (Isa. 66:2)

Fidelity like that to the God who cares for us so deeply is thus rewarded and comforted:

> Rejoice with Jerusalem and be glad for her,
> all you who love her;
> rejoice greatly with her,
> all you who mourn over her.
> For you will nurse and be satisfied
> at her comforting breasts;
> you will drink deeply
> and delight in her overflowing abundance.
> (Isa. 66:10–11)

He assures us that after the pain comes the joy for all who are faithful to him:

> I will extend peace to her like a river,
> and the wealth of nations like a flooding stream;
> you will nurse and be carried on her arm
> and dandled on her knees.
> As a mother comforts her child,
> so will I comfort you;
> and you will be comforted over Jerusalem.
> When you see this, your heart will rejoice
> and you will flourish like grass. (Isa. 66:12–14)

My hope is that weary hearts will be lifted up to recognise how *precious* we are to God. By reflecting on God's plans of love for His people – erring though we may be or have been – we too will recognise the tenderness of God who draws us 'with reins of kindness and love'. We too will take courage and look at our own infidelities, but learn to turn to our God with gratitude and hope because our God is 'wonderful and full of compassion'.

God's greatest delight, however, is always in his Beloved Son, Jesus Christ. We hope to see this when we reflect on the Incarnation, which is the central point of our spirituality. As St. Paul says: 'There is only Christ; he is everything; he is in everything' (Col. 3:11).

A Chance to Reflect

- *Your word, Lord, in scripture is sacred. To think that I can hear it spoken to me, in my life circumstances, if I truly listen and let myself be taught by You. Slow my pace, Lord, I'm too hasty at times.*
- *You want to be my saving rock, Lord, but I need to co-operate by listening, by being open and honest, by depending on You and having an open and grateful heart.*
- *I know that one of my weaknesses is that I take my own pace not the pace of Your Spirit. Please slow me down, Lord, or I will miss Your teaching. That means I will not be a cause of delight to You. It is so easy to delight You by being obedient to what You are letting me see is the way to go, because it is there I meet You in love.*
- *Waiting . . . this is difficult, I know. I fail often here. Sometimes I have become distracted and missed what You were teaching me! At other times, I wanted to move more quickly than You! What a foolish thing to do! At other times, I liked being in control! Have pity on me, Lord. Stay with me!*
- *I see that I need to pray for an increase of faith and hope and love. Then I need to practise these virtues in daily life,*

and to meet You and delight You in the doing of that. For example, if I had a problem, I see that if I prayed to look at things from Your point of view, I would be praying for a living faith. That would be something alive, not dead. I could do the same with hope and love. Help me to do that, Lord. I can also ask myself whether my faith, my hope, my love are in line with what You want for me. If it draws me closer to You, then I'm on target. If it draws me away from You, then I'm not in harmony with You any more. Thank You, Lord, for Your teaching.

- *You speak to me in various ways. Am I always a good listener and a loving disciple? I'm afraid not!*
- *There is so much in this chapter on scripture, I need to break it up and move slowly. By now, I could help myself more perhaps. What is each of the prophets saying? Which of them touches me most? Why?*

A Chance to Pray

I thank you, Lord, for speaking to me, unworthy though I am. I can get carried away and forget to praise, glorify and thank You. Let me practise saying frequently: 'Glory be to the Father, and to the Son, and to the Holy Spirit. As it was in the beginning, is now and ever shall be, world without end. Amen.'

Jesus, help me to choose just one verse of
scripture each day. For example, hearing
You say to me: 'You are precious to me.'
Help me to glorify You by just that verse.
First let me thank You for saying it to me;
increase my faith and my hope and my love.

Then, help me to understand that each person is precious to You. Let me rejoice in that truth. Let me apply it to my own life – especially where X is concerned, X whom I do not like! Heal my unkindness and open my heart to Your word of scripture. Thank you, Jesus.

4

THE TITLE – A GIFT OF LOVE

The title of this book, 'God's Delight', is closely connected with desert retreats. I will talk in greater detail later about desert retreats and how they began. At the moment, let me say that seven of us had come together to seek God alone. We chose to live as simply as possible to try to come 'naked' before Almighty God. Therefore, we chose not to have the usual supports in a retreat: we had no director, no scripture, no Eucharist, no extra reading, no resting in the presence of the Blessed Sacrament, nothing except being present to God, waiting on His lead, His plan for each of us, His word or His total silence, whatever He chose . . .

This was the third desert retreat I had set up as a response to God's call. Those who are invited come each time as a result of much prayer and discernment. In this particular retreat, we had quite a high-powered ecumenical group. Without naming people, I can say that each had a full role in God's Church. There were three clergymen – a Cistercian Austrian priest deeply involved with inspiring youth, at great cost to himself;

an Anglican priest; a Roman Catholic priest – a layman (co-founder of a Spirit-filled movement of international status); a retired doctor who, as a linguist, translates St Augustine and various Vatican documents into Spanish and French for her lay institute; my colleague who carries a full-time job in a hospital yet spearheads spirituality training for the laity through 'Light Out of Darkness', as well as other ecumenical activities; and myself.

I mention these people because the only activity we engage in together in the desert retreat is faith-sharing. For me, therefore, to share the following experience of God with such a group before we had thoroughly gelled was a formidable challenge. I knew, however, that their reaction would be the acid test! It would be clear confirmation or total rejection. I knew I should do this and very soon I came to a place of peace.

During this third desert retreat, we used to pray in our bedrooms, in the grounds of our retreat house, or in a large, barn-like room which served us for our simple meals with a small section cut off for private prayer. This is where I sat one morning on a hard chair, intending to stay there from 11.00 a.m. to 12.00 midday. I was not surprised at the great dryness that at first gripped me. This could be expected, as I had discovered in two former retreats. I kept my attention fixed, as well as I could, on a large crucifix, grateful that I hadn't suggested removing it too! I remember when my thoughts turned to Jesus and to how little I was giving Him. Behind me, in a corner, was one of the priests whom I know well, and whose commitment to God is sincere and deep. I began offering to Jesus the love and devotion and prayer of this priest, to praise and glorify God, and to make amends for my own coldness and lack of warmth and fervour.

Then, quite suddenly, it happened. It is so difficult to put into words something like this which is beyond my understanding.

My bleak isolation was suddenly broken by a kind of swishing sound – heard interiorly. It resembled the movement of water; it seemed to fill up my being. Then I became aware of another accompanying sound, like perhaps a smothered joy-filled sound – laughter is too strong, yet it held laughter – it was more like a delight-filled breath, yet not quite that. I was startled. I heard myself asking interiorly: 'What's all this? What's going on here?' I knew I wasn't afraid, but I did not understand! Then I heard very clearly within my being: 'This is God's delight.' I said: 'What! What is going on?' Then came the joy-filled sound again and the words resounding within me: **'This is God's delight because you have let Me use you to bring My people together.'**

Much later, when I was led to reflect more deeply on this, I recognised that these words were the first part of a three-fold message.

At that time, in the barn, these words were followed at once by a vividly clear picture. Jesus held our little group in a circle in His arms. He was touching each one of us, and yet His arms, while embracing us, reached out at the same time way beyond us. I still see the beauty of His long fingers, stretching out and out . . . seeking to reach and to touch!

Again in my later reflection, I understood this to indicate how God longs to gather all His people to Him and how delighted He is when each one of us allows ourself to be at His disposal, to use as He wills, so as to serve His Body, and to be served by the other members of His Body.

At that time, in the barn, it seemed that this picture was followed immediately by my saying excitedly: 'But how do we celebrate? We have no paten.'

I was, of course, thinking traditionally, and instinctively thought of the Eucharist celebration as fitting. Jesus again smiled and with that indescribable sound, not laughter, more like a gentle musical chuckle, said: 'What's wrong with My heart?!' And so it seemed very appropriate and natural for me to lift each one of our group and place us all in His heart.

Again on later reflection on the whole experience and praying for light, I understood the first words to be His expression of delight that I was His willing instrument, to be used by Him in whatever way He wanted, to reach His people. The picture of us as a group held close to Him, through whom He was able to reach out to His other children, spoke strongly to me of His Body, through which He continues to speak to us today. Finally, His holding us all in His heart spoke to me of the importance of love, our love for Him and for His Body, and His love binding us all together, empowering us to do His will.

(This emphasis on His love, which He wants to keep pouring over us, has been confirmed for me many times since and reached a high point in the Holy Land at the site of the Primacy of Peter.)

It came to the third morning of our desert retreat. It was time for me to share this experience with the other six members. At our faith-sharing session, I waited until last, as I didn't want to risk spoiling the sharing for anyone else, when I told my story. I need not have been at all anxious. On a desert retreat, it is our custom never to speak except to do our own faith-sharing. Neither do we comment on the sharing of anyone else. The faces, however, of the six, their expressions, the light in their eyes, were clear affirmation for me! Then suddenly, contrary to custom, one of them spoke: **'Let us gather together in a circle, holding each other as Jesus held us, and let us pray silently for all His people.'**

That was a memorable moment of presence of God and union with one another!

This forgotten or repressed experience came back to me crystal-clear three weeks after my meeting with those who suggested another book. This time, instead of 'What's wrong with My heart?', I heard: 'What's wrong with "God's Delight"?' and knew I had got the *title* of the book He wanted.

A keen testing followed – powerlessness, lack of energy, lack of the usual zest for living. Now, months later, with restored health, it seems like a dream. I would not be without that experience, however; I had too much to learn! More than ever I feel that God is not loved as He longs to be loved by us, His children. This response from us is what constitutes His greatest delight. His greatest longing is to be for us the **Way**, the **Truth** and the **Life**. This is how we can best grow into the image of God that we are and are called to become. It requires from us, however, an emptying of certain securities, our strong positions, our gifts that have to date carried us on, successfully perhaps, even in ministry. As I said before, God is a jealous God! He loves us so much that He wants to fill us with Himself. He wants us to breathe with His breath, to see with His vision, to love with His heart; all of course is impossible for us, but if God finds our hearts ready, He is ready to work miracles, in His way, in His time, to fulfil His purposes.

This is the meaning of His **Incarnation** which is **the heart of this book**. He empties Himself to show us the Way. He teaches us through His humanity. Later, as Risen Lord, through His Spirit, He teaches us **the Truth** that we must follow. Thus we begin to share His Risen Life, to open our own humanity more, to be transformed by His presence within us – teaching us, leading us, inspiring us to be, to think, to act as the Lord God desires us to do. **He Himself is the Life**.

A Chance to Reflect

Let us pause, Lord, before we move on to Your Incarnation.

- *Help me to discern, in this silence, where we are in this relationship of love; help me to desire You more, day by day. Show me, please, where You hope I will make some changes and teach me how to delight You more.*
- *Let me learn to discern the movement of Your Spirit in my life; help me to banish fear and to listen more deeply to Your voice. Teach me, Lord, that when I seek You with*

all my heart, You speak and I can hear, You move and I can recognize that it is You. This is Your gift to us.

A Chance to Pray

Jesus, this is a sacred time for us. It needs to be a private, silent time . . . a time for lovers. Stay with me, Lord, that I may rest in Your presence, full of trust. Focus me, Lord, on You alone, on Your love for us all, on Your desire to use each of us for others. Lord, help me to recognise the privilege of being a member of Your Body. Here I am, Lord, take me, teach me, strengthen my weakness, increase my love for You, and for my sisters and brothers.

Jesus, my heart is too narrow, too small. You want to broaden my vision and open my heart wide, so that You can place within it all the people You want me to carry in love. Only You can do this, Jesus. Give me Your own heart to love You with; make me humble and gentle like you; let me turn nobody away from finding rest and peace in my heart.

INCARNATION

A Mystery of Love

Late it was that I loved You, beauty so ancient and yet so new, late I loved you. And look, You were within me and I was in the world outside myself. I searched for you outside myself and, disfigured as I was, I fell upon the beautiful things of Your creation. You were with me and I was not with You. The beautiful things of this world kept me far from You and yet, if they had not been in You, they would not have existed at all. You called me, You cried aloud to me, You broke my barrier of deafness, You shone upon me, Your radiance enveloped me, You put my blindness to flight. You breathed fragrance, and I drew in my breath and now I gasp for You. I tasted You and now I am hungry and thirsty for You. You touched me and I burned for Your peace.

St Augustine (Confessions 10,27)

5

INCARNATION – FORGOTTEN, MISUNDERSTOOD OR ALIVE?

So far, we have perhaps experienced a little of God's delight in us, His children; hopefully we have experienced and been refreshed by His unchanging love for us; His own word in scripture has in it life, strength and renewal which no doubt has reached us and confirmed our experience. We have read and seen how God's love and humility bend down to us to use us for His purposes, if we wish to use the gifts He has given to each of us: eyes to see, ears to hear and be taught, hearts to open and be filled with His own life.

We come now to the heart of this book, which is Incarnation. In this opening chapter, I wish to give in general terms the intent of God, contrasting it with our life at the end of this twentieth century as we glimpsed it earlier; I give also an experience of vibrant incarnational living contrasted with a desert barrenness. In our lives, we must *choose* which we truly want. That is the awesome dignity, grandeur, freedom of Christianity. We are loved with an unchanging love by a God who gives us everything, but our *free response in love* is the choice we must make, so as to delight Him.

Our relationship with God and His with us is meant to be a continual love-story. This love-story becomes a daily transformation of our darkness and weakness into the light and the strength of God. Even when our response to Him is totally inadequate, is indeed rejection at times, even then God's love for us remains unchanged. He will never forsake us; He cannot, He will not, because His very essence is love. Almighty God **is Love**.

This is why the story of our salvation is 'rooted and planted in love' (Eph. 3:17), the love that is God. He has *first* loved us – our response to that love, in the Holy Spirit and by His power, becomes more real, when our hearts are genuine.

Our human response to salvation

It is time, I think, that we take a good look at the whole question of our response to the mystery of salvation. What is its basic quality? We have talked about our relationship being a love-story, but that means that we, as well as God, are fully committed. Are we?

Is it not true to say that when we think of salvation, we see – yet without truly seeing – that Jesus Christ has died for us, has given us His life so that we are saved and redeemed from the power of the enemy. Allied to that, however, is it not also true, at least for some of the time, that we tend to think of salvation in terms of the minimum on our part – that is, getting by, scraping into heaven, not being condemned to hell! Is that response conducive to a fully alive relationship of love which deserves the name? Is that response a delight to Him?

It is time to be honest and to face facts. God is a great

lover, a passionate God who spares nothing, gives all, to woo us to a response that matches His. We who are created in His image have the same potential of loving within us. We are **not** God, but God, by living within us through the Holy Spirit of Love, empowers us to become 'like unto Him'. *That is the meaning of His Incarnation in the flesh and His continuing Incarnation in our humanity today.* We are called to respond as passionate lovers of the King of Love, who, knowing our weakness, takes over our life, our every breath, our ability to love, and gives us Himself. A wonderful exchange – if we are willing.

Listen to St Paul: 'I have been crucified with Christ and I no longer live, but Christ lives in me. The life I live in the body, I live by faith in the Son of God, who loved me and gave himself for me' (Gal. 2:20).

In human terms, we know that genuine lovers who live for one another – not selfishly putting self-interest first – begin to grow like one another. Because of love, they try to enter into the mind, the heart and the desires of the other. Since both do this, the inevitable happens. Through the continuous transcendence of selfish interests, they meet in a new place, a place where self has died and mutual love has received new life, new growth. God has brought them 'out into a spacious place . . . because he delighted in them' (Ps. 18:19).

It is clear, of course, that love drew them *to die to self* so as *to rise to this new life*. It is also clear that the power of Jesus Christ, **the Way, the Truth and the Life**, was living deeply within these human lovers. An ideal picture, of course; the trouble with us today is that we seem to have weakened on ideals!

God's love as manifested in salvation

Let us now look at the Godhead, the Three-in-One, the Father, Son and Spirit, the Infinite and Passionate Lovers, who have created us.

Incarnation itself is a *mystery of love* which involves the whole Trinity. The whole human race – images of God – was in deadly peril. Incarnation was the emptying of the Second Person, the Word Eternal, of divine trappings so that in becoming one of us humans, He could accomplish our salvation through loving. Only infinite love within the Trinity, and for all of us, could overcome the hate of the enemy. And so it happened. The infinite love within the Trinity covered us in *salvific love* and does so to the end of time, that we may know life eternal in its fullness in God. The Holy Spirit expresses as Third Person of the Trinity, the *mutual love* of Father for Son and Son for Father. The cost to the Trinity of this plan of self-emptying of the Son, so as to become visible love in the flesh, is as infinite as their love.

The Son is 'the chosen one in whom the Father delights' (Isa. 42:1–4), the One who in His humanity is 'the servant' who commits Himself to the total fulfilment of the Father's plan for our salvation. To this degree does the Father love us: He sends His well-beloved Son to ransom us *at the cost of His own life*. We are ransomed so that we can live and be co-heirs to the kingdom. The price is the Passion and death of the Son whom He loves.

When the Son joins the sinners in the Jordan to be baptised, the Son is proclaiming His understanding and full acceptance of the plan of the Godhead: as Son of God, He takes on the burden of the sin of His brothers and sisters that we are; all sin is the rejection of love, so only the Son of God, who is love, can bear the weight of this burden and transform *death into life,* transform rejection of love – sin – into the fullness of love, **God's love**.

To proclaim this mystery of love at such a time, in such a way, can only be done by the Trinity, Three Persons yet One in essence. The Three are present and active at the Jordan, where humility and abasement are transformed into glory and joy. God the Father speaks: 'This is my Son, whom I love; with him I am well pleased' (Matt. 3:17). God the Son is baptised; God the Holy Spirit descends like a dove and lights on Him. **Love fills the earth**.

Still later at the Transfiguration of Jesus on the mountain in the presence of three of the disciples, we are given a brief glimpse of the *true glory* of the King of Kings. This special revelation of the divinity of Jesus is the Father's divine affirmation of everything Jesus has done and is about to do, in and through His Passion and death. While Peter was foolishly speaking at a time when silent worship and awe were appropriate 'a bright cloud enveloped them, and a voice from the cloud said: "This is my Son whom I love; with him I am well pleased. Listen to him!"' (Matt. 17:5).

'Listen to My Son' is the word of God the Father to us, God's children, and His message is the very heart of Incarnation, namely love. 'My Son whom I love.' It is to Jesus, His Son, who is *fully human* that we are to listen. Why? What has Jesus to tell us that is so special that we are to listen to Him according to the command of His Father in heaven? **Jesus is Love made visible on earth!** Jesus *is* love; Jesus is Emmanuel, God-with-us, because Love urged Him to come to save us – through love. The *means* is His life in Nazareth, His ministry, and His Passion and death, but the *power* is the saving power of love. Because we do not let God love us – being so busy about proving to God that we love Him and are therefore good and worthy! – we are not really in touch with the power of love, which is God's love. The power of God's loving us and our receiving it transforms our very being. We are a little afraid perhaps of being transformed, changed? It is outside our control. It might be too much! 'O foolish and slow of heart to believe' says Jesus to you, to me, as He once said it on the road to Emmaus to other disciples. Do we want to risk not meeting Jesus on our journey? To miss our unique love-relationship with Him? Can we be so foolish, so lacking in trust? Then let the Spirit of Love fan into a flame the precious gift of love we already have. Let *human* love teach us; let our response to other humans draw us deeper into the depths of God's own love.

Love experience of new life

Let me share with you an experience of **God's transforming love** active in an ordinary situation.

I was invited to talk at a pre-Advent ecumenical meeting on the theme of 'Inner Light'. My undoing was the theme. I felt drawn there, unable to resist, although pressure was mounting at that time, which is something not unknown to any of us. As weariness increased, as nerves jangled, as mind blanked out, I froze within my being. What kind of a fool was I to travel some distance, to address people I had never met, who probably were not keen on an Irish, Roman Catholic religious coming to talk to them on 'Inner Light'. Darkness was closer to me, as I set out.

Worse still! When I had awakened that morning and was becoming present to the Lord at the beginning of a new day, I thought also of this coming ecumenical meeting. I felt miserable. I was empty. 'Inner Light' as a

theme had lost all its attraction, devoid of warmth. I cried out to the Lord, asking for help, for light, and if possible not to have to go at all. I knew in my heart that I was being childish, that God would not let me or His people down, but I needed to have my little moan and groan!

At the time, I was writing on Incarnation. A first draft. It was not too difficult nor surprising to hear the voice of God chiding me and saying: 'Why not Incarnation?' Why not indeed, except that it had to fit into the given theme of 'Inner Light' and my mind remained blank. However, a spark had lit. 'Incarnation' now caught me and I joined my helplessness with that of the child in the manger. God was for us, so who could be against us?

I recall that evening with amazement. Once again, I discovered how God uses us, one for another, in such a power-filled way. He is so present in His Body. He was asking me to trust Him, to let go the obstacle of my *fear*, my need to speak well and not to let the side down. As soon as I stepped inside the door, the welcoming bright faces of the organisers cheered me. It was the Body of Christ in action. As people arrived, I felt filled, somehow, by their very presence, with an overpowering experience of God's love. Their openness dissolved all darkness; the light within me shone more brightly by reason of God's clear presence. All I had to do was to be led by Him, to let Him give whatever He wanted both myself and the listeners to hear. God was in charge and I had given up control. I remained in His presence, listening to the eagerness and love that lit so many faces – their inner light was drawing me along the way. I became conscious of inner light, inner warmth, inner power within myself, within the group. It flowed, it poured out, as if God could not restrain Himself. It was all so simple, so very simple, but He was with us. 'I delight to be with the children of men' (Ps. 149:4). Scripture was fulfilled that evening. He used us for one another.

At the end of forty minutes, I felt very confident about inviting people, who were not well-known to each other and who had never done faith-sharing in groups, to take a space to reflect on what God had said to them *individually*. Those who were willing shared with the large group. This was truly feeding one another. Quietly, at the end, one old lady – who I'm sure was younger than myself – gave me a gift which I treasure: she whispered, 'When I come to die, I pray to God that I will have the light of God shining from my face then, as you have had it tonight.' And I had been anxious about going there! 'O, you of little faith . . .' (Matt. 6:30; 8:26).

A contrasting experience

Next morning, I was still enveloped in this wonderful love of God which had happened among strangers, and I knew that I had been greatly graced by being among all those people of God. I wanted to share it. I walked through a street in a nearby town. I smiled at people, I looked at them with all the love in my heart, but I seemed to be thrown from the furnace of God's love into an icy-cold desert region. It was a shocking, a traumatic change! I wanted to set alight the inner glow through kindly feelings, through sharing, as had happened on the previous night. The morning air was brisk and invigorating. My heart had been singing, a smile in my heart and eyes lit with welcome . . . A blank sea of faces, dead, seeing nothing, nobody, **hit me** with sharp, piercing coldness: hard expressions, hurt eyes, tight lips, open wounds, closed hearts, bitterness, hostility . . . I stumbled on . . . there had to be someone . . . in the distance I saw an acquaintance . . . I did not really know her, except that when she was in business she had been friendly . . . now she was retired . . .

I greeted her cheerfully, got little response; I persevered and found that she was glad she had retired, life was not what it used to be, people had no longer time for one another . . . She was filled with a horror story of the previous day when an elderly woman was savaged by two young people – for seventy-four pence; my acquaintance was traumatised . . . I tried in vain to share with her a little of the good news of the previous night, and the goodwill I had experienced. She was polite but didn't hear what I said, she was not interested. I felt useless; it was not the right time for her, nor was I the right person. I could only cry in my heart for the pain of God's people and for the pain of God which was still continuing in us and in so many places. I could only beg Him to send someone to my friend of the street, to help lift her burden which I was unable to do. I could only hold the street in prayer, begging for the presence and action of the Spirit. I recognised how easy it is for all of us to wear a dark face instead of letting God's light and love fill His world.

The first experience was vibrant, incarnational living. It lit up for me what can happen when we let go and let the love of God take over. Then we have time for one another, then we can give life to one another. But as free people, we must make the choice. **It all happens in our ordinary daily encounters**. The second scene revealed too clearly what can happen if we shut out God from our daily lives. The hardness of heart which begins in our inner self-love spreads to indifference to others. Eventually indifference to others can result in an inner deadness which becomes corpse-like.

What can we do?

Christ loves us so much and wants to pour out love that will heal us. He longs to fill us with inner peace and radiance. It is why He became incarnate for us. We are the *new Jerusalem*; He had wept over the old Jerusalem, while longing to save and hold her in love . . . but she 'would not', nor at times 'would' we. Do we want Christ to continue weeping over us, or do we want Him to be our Saviour? What can we do?

'Listen to My Son.'

John of the Cross had listened well to Christ the Saviour. He learnt and he expressed it thus: 'Put love where there is no love and you will find love.' That works; I've tried it repeatedly and yes, it works. It means surrendering oneself in whatever way the circumstances demand, but it works. I can gain more inner light, inner insight, inner strength by putting love where I found none, even if it appears to have no result, as with my acquaintance on the street. Someone else will bring that seed to life. This is how He saves us – by love. Sometimes it is our love for others that is His instrument; more frequently it is the love of others reaching to us and touching us which heals. Let us not waste God's love. Let us begin by loving ourselves, letting His love of us melt our hearts so that we love ourselves *with His love*. He then lets His love in us touch other hearts. Thus He uses us to let ripples of God-love flow into us and through us, while simultaneously, ripples of His love flow to us from others. It is all God's work. We co-operate by eagerly desiring to be filled with His infinite love and to be used as channels of life for others.

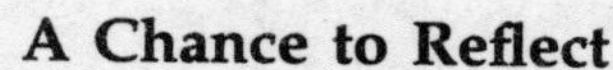

A Chance to Reflect

The process of salvation is essentially a love-story between God and myself.

- *In this two-sided love-story, am I being honest? Do I desire perhaps to give more? God is listening and eager to help, but I have to make a move!*
- *Scripture tells us that God is a jealous God – not in a self-centred, possessive, destructive way, as we sinners behave at times. 'The Lord your God is a consuming fire, a jealous God' (Deut. 4:24). We cannot serve two masters, God and Mammon! Thus He continues to save us.*
- *In human relations, letting go can be a true sign of giving all to the loved one. The Trinity's love is a God-giving sharing of their very life.*
- *At the Jordan and again at the Transfiguration, Christ's humanity and divinity come together. Both reveal the totality of His giving. We tend to count the cost!*
- *Emmanuel, God-with-us, became a transforming power at the ecumenical meeting described here. Faith, hope and love were the human factors that released the action of the Spirit. Can street-scenes be likewise transformed?*

A Chance to Pray

(silently or in simple words . . . perhaps:)

Come, Lord Jesus, into this situation.
We are helpless, come and open our eyes, our hearts,
melt us, mould us.
We praise You and thank You
and glorify You, Emmanuel.

6

INCARNATION – THE HIDDEN LIFE

The people who walked in darkness have seen a
great light;
those who dwelt in a land of deep darkness, on them
has light shined;
Thou hast multiplied the nation, thou hast increased
its joy;
they rejoice before thee as with joy at the harvest,
as men rejoice when they divide the spoil.
For the yoke of his burden,
and the staff of his shoulder,
the rod of his oppressor,
thou hast broken as on the day of Midian.
For every boot of the tramping warrior in battle
tumult
and every garment rolled in blood will be burned
as fuel for the fire.
For to us a child is born,
to us a son is given.

(Isa. 9:2–6)

INCARNATION – THE HIDDEN LIFE

The birth of Jesus Christ, the coming of the Eternal Word, God, eternal, without a beginning or an end, **eternal**, vulnerable, dependent, *becoming human like you and me*, why? . . . because He loves us!

If we do not grasp the true meaning of Incarnation – the Word becoming flesh in the womb of a creature of God – we will not understand the depth of God's mad folly, the length to which He will go to save you, to save me, because **our salvation** is what all this pain, all this forsaking the glory of His state, all this dying, being mocked, scourged and crucified is about . . . He loves us so passionately that all His life is an experience of the pain of loving, culminating in the Passion.

If we do not try to grasp *the radical Way* which Jesus followed *the stark, yet life-giving Truth* He experienced in His humanity, so that He could teach us with the authority of having personally lived it, we won't understand the kind of *Life* He has won for us, the eternal life for which He has redeemed us, the life of the Trinity which He wants to share with us eternally. If we do not grasp the meaning of all this loving, then what response can we make? *The love-story will remain one-sided.*

We are so circumscribed by the limitations of our humanity, and, worse, by the false perceptions of our sinfulness, that for us, alone, it is futile, it is impossible even to dream of the meaning of a life eternal. The poverty of our vision, the hardness of our heart, the contamination of our best desires leave us, in fact, questioning at times whether it is worth the effort! The life of pleasure has sapped our best effort, our desire, our inspiration. The exhilaration of vision has lost out to commonplace seeing and weighing the newest commodity. Exploration, risking, adventure for the joy of it, for the challenging fulfilment of the precious uniqueness that is a person, has been sold for less than thirty pieces of silver in the market-place, or is it in the Temple?

Only a God who is Truth, a God who knows the crazy, deceptive path that opens up for us, only a God who values us more than His own life, can love us to death, can keep the door wide open, longing to hear our eager footsteps, or laggard ones, or last-minute returning ones. Such a God will surely suffer. Such a God keeps us always in mind, supporting our weak intent, meeting us while we are still coming . . . it is why He came.

There is a Second Coming in the offing. When? We do not know. But our human life experience surely tells us that if we do not learn from our mistakes, we will not reform on the morrow.

This mystery of love which is the Incarnation of the Word made flesh does not end with Calvary when His human flesh died as He surrendered His Spirit to God the Father. In Christ's rising in the Spirit, He continues this mystery of Incarnation, **the Risen Christ incarnate today in our human flesh**. It is the same mystery of love but in a different form. The historical Jesus of Nazareth stands in His Resurrection at the right hand of the Father, flooding the world and us with the fullness of the Holy Spirit. Through this Spirit, Christ's Incarnation today is the life of the Risen Christ within us, making us whole, saving us by enlightening us as to the **Way** to go, the **Truth** to follow and the **Life** to lead, so that all within us is transformed and becomes more truly the image of God that we are. The plan of God is eternal.

Incarnation is therefore a mystery, but seen in human terms, it stretches to the end of all time when human life is no more, and Christ the Saviour has brought us to 'the measure of all the fullness of God'. Contrast that electrifying truth with the poverty of today's trend of identifying 'incarnation' with the highly commercialised period of the Christmas festivities. The eternal plan of God was put into effect when Mary, His Mother, said her 'fiat' to God's invitation through the Angel Gabriel, and God became visible on earth.

> Do not be afraid, Mary, you have found favour with God. You will be with child and give birth to a son, and you are to give him the name Jesus. He will be great and will be called the Son of the Most High . . . The Holy Spirit will come upon you and the power of the Most High will overshadow you. So the holy one to be born will be called the Son of God.
>
> (Luke 1:30–35)

Let Jesus be truly human

If we refuse to let Jesus be human, like us in all things – sin alone excepted – we are denying to Him the fullness of the 'emptying process' which He experienced for us. And we ourselves, consciously or unconsciously, will tend to hide from the reality that confronts us, that for love of us, He gave up all the trappings of divinity. At no time did Jesus enjoy special privileges or advantages. On earth, Jesus worked within the terms of His humanity. He had to learn from His own *personal* experience all that was involved in being a human being. He had never been incarnate in human flesh before! Everything was a first-time experience and must at times have been painful, excruciating learning.

Our personal experience of being human

We sometimes take our human experience for granted and in doing so, we can fail to grow through it to the degree that is possible. Jesus, we are told in scripture, advanced in 'wisdom, age and grace'. That option is also open to us, if we value the gift of our humanity. All gifts come from God! With Jesus, we share the same Spirit, by whom we are led if we will. We will begin with our own humanity, so that in looking later at the humanity of Christ, we will be better prepared to see what we share as human beings with Jesus Christ. We will also see where we missed what could have given delight to the God who created us.

It is now widely accepted in psychological and spiritual circles that growth in the human and spiritual dimensions begins first with our getting to know the truth of who we are. Knowing the truth of ourselves involves the recognition that we are sinners. We learn, however, that we are also loved by God – and hopefully loved also by parents, immediate and perhaps extended family. Human love is truly a necessary foundation for divine love. The visible mediates more easily the truth of the invisible.

Encouraged by love, we move to being able to recognise our dark areas, to claim them, to claim responsibility for them and to look towards the light which can transform them. The light in human terms may manifest itself in approval, warmth, support. In spiritual terms, this gradually becomes an awareness of a sense of well-being or ease, or peace with God or with Jesus.

The effect of darkness being transformed into light, even in small matters, is the beginning of a *liberation process* which leads to maturity. This process of darkness being seen against the light, being claimed and surrendered and transformed, which facilitates our becoming daily more free, more in harmony with God and with people, is what we mean by **salvation**.

It is all God's work, but we are co-workers. It proceeds, no matter how small the darkness or the light may be; however small the steps we take, the vital part is that we allow God's action to be fruitful by our co-operation. Thus we, like Jesus, grow in wisdom, as human beings. The difference of course is that *we* advance from darkness into light, all the days of our life, because we advance into infinite light. Jesus was advancing into deeper awareness of human life, of His own experience and that of others; He encountered sinners and the darker side of life as an experience which belonged to others but deeply moved Him to compassion. He also advanced into awareness of His identity as Saviour, as Light of the World, and of His mission; above all, He advanced in the wisdom resulting from His relationship with His Father.

Our moving from darkness into light is a slow experience and at times costs a great deal of pain, of sorrow, of anxiety, of weakness. It is necessary for us to take the pace of God's Spirit, as our natural frailty – compounded of fear, ambition, pride, over-zeal – can expose us to weariness, impatience, arrogance, absence of humility and truth. The 'liberating' process continues, however, and the strengthening gift of the Spirit comes when we are taught by the Spirit that we are God's true delight when we place our hope in Him! (Ps.147:11). Thus we can advance still more surely when we let the awareness of God's Spirit acting within us fill us with hope, joy and delight!

When we are trying to delight God, we will begin to be aware of a growing sense of peace within us. This spiritual well-being is signalled by the lifting of our focus from self to God or to others. This healthy movement is energising in the spiritual sense. Fidelity to listening to the Spirit and obeying His prompting leads us into greater freedom still. Such freedom accelerates our longing to love God and to come closer to Him. This gift of freedom implies a change of attitude, of values, of direction; it implies a softening of the heart, a letting go of one's self-interest, a greater concern with the neighbour, a growing concern about God's care for His people allied with a sense of deeper intimacy with God Himself. In time, this deeper relationship with the God of love gives rise to a more real 'knowing of oneself', a knowing that does not disturb, even when the knowing is a discovery of hidden frailty or darkness. What matters at this stage is not darkness or light but the God who is Light! It is a new depth of freedom which kindles an awareness of 'a new thing' being done by the Spirit, with the intent of kindling the whole Body. **And all this is the delight of God**.

To live as Christ would have us live can be costly, but how rewarding! It cost Him thirty years of incarnation as a human being with all that was involved in that experience. This is the only Way that enriches, that lifts us out of the valley and places us on a mountain-top. Moreover, we are never alone; even in this world, the intimacy and union can begin through the power of His Spirit of Love. Scripture tells us the 'good news':

> I tell you the truth, you will weep and mourn while the world rejoices. You will grieve, but your grief will turn into joy. A woman giving birth to a child has pain because her time has come; but when her baby is born she forgets the anguish because of her joy that a child is born into the world. (John 16:20–21)

For us sinners, the process of slow transformation happens through our continuous surrender to the daily birth pangs, the problems, our letting the Spirit have more space within our hearts to allow Christ to live within us. Then the pain is forgotten in the ensuing joy of our new life. It is all the work of the Spirit in us and Christ sent us the Spirit when He had completed His human experience on earth.

Christ's personal experience of humanity

Can I conceive of myself freely choosing – for the love of anyone – to become one of a lower species of life, an animal, a bird, an insect? Yet I myself am a creature too, the work of the hands of the Creator, as are animals, birds, insects.

I am not the creator or maker of animals, birds or insects, as Christ, the Son of God the Father, the Creator, is. If I had to depend on this 'lower life-form' to help me live, to supply food and drink, to help me crawl or fly, or clamber up trees, whatever this new mode of life demanded, I could perhaps begin to understand the 'emptying process' more realistically; and yet even then, it is a far cry from the situation of Jesus of Nazareth, *Son of God*:

> Who, being in very nature God,

did not consider equality with God something to be
grasped,
but made himself nothing,
taking the very nature of a servant,
being made in human likeness.
And being found in appearance as a man,
he humbled himself
and became obedient to death – even death on a
cross! (Phil. 2:6–8)

Christ's identity

At what stage did Christ come to the truth of who He really was? I do not know. I favour the school that lets Him be truly human, discovering all the facets of that experience as humans do; what did His Mother understand, and what did Elizabeth's greeting mean to her? I prefer to let Christ be the dependent infant in the manger, helpless, responsive to the variations of adult emotions: the excitement of the shepherds, their great joy, the singing of the angels – told to Jesus at a later stage; the meeting in the temple with Simeon, at His Presentation according to the Law, and the words which brought first joy and then shock to His Mother and Joseph, requiring 'deep pondering':

Sovereign Lord, as you have promised,
you now dismiss your servant in peace.
For my eyes have seen your salvation,
which you have prepared in the sight of all people,
a light for revelation to the Gentiles
and for glory to your people, Israel.

Then Simeon blessed them and said to Mary, his

> Mother: 'This child is destined to cause the falling and rising of many in Israel, and to be a sign that will be spoken against, so that the thoughts of many hearts will be revealed. And a sword will pierce your own soul too.' (Luke 2:29–35).

Any sword that would pierce His Mother's soul would be also a piercing of Christ's soul.

The visit of the Magi precipitated, through the jealousy and hatred of Herod, the heartbreak of the massacre of the Holy Innocents. These were the first of a long line who died so that the Christ would live, that in His own dying for us all, the redemptive plan of the Trinity would be accomplished. And so the pain of life encompassed Him from birth.

From the start of His human experience, Christ was familiar with suffering, the human experience that taught Him obedience. Obedience is a love-word, a love-attitude, a love-action, a love-response, or it is nothing but sadism or masochism. God's plan of salvation through sending Christ on earth was a **Trinitarian plan of love**. I can only use human words to express what we cannot know – the mind of God. God the Father's love for his Son was the total outpouring of Himself to the Son; the Father's sending this beloved Son into our world was, therefore, at great cost to the Father; the cost to the Son we let scripture present and help us to begin to understand. Yet the letting go of the trappings of divinity was only a beginning. Christ's joy and love and reverence that pours out of Him in discovering His Father reveals, especially in St John (chapters 14, 15, 17), a glimpse of what the deprivation of their 'togetherness' meant to Christ.

Nazareth: I have always been intrigued by the thirty years spent in Nazareth. Just a few lines in scripture, no more. So hidden was it all! His experience in the Temple at the age of Twelve must have been a giant leap for Him into discovering His identity. 'Why were you searching for me?' was His response to the Mother He loved, with whom He must have reflected often upon the meaning of the early 'strange' happenings, as well as the daily insights into which He was led by the Spirit. 'Didn't you know I had to be in *my Father's house*?' Was this an insight that was given to Him at the moment His Mother mentioned their searching for Him; 'Your *father* and I have been anxiously searching for you', or was it confirmation of a growing awareness? Was this his first sounding out of saying aloud 'My Father' contrasting with the more familiar 'fatherhood' of Joseph? At any rate, it was all a new and perhaps startling experience. And then 'He went down to Nazareth with them and was obedient to them' (Luke 2:51). Such fidelity, such obedience, such love for God, His Father, and for all of us.

In this painful searching for His identity, we must never lose sight of the fact that discovering His identity as the Son of God meant, for Him, at the same time, a growing awareness of His mission and the responsibility of being Messiah. This was an unparalleled burden, willing though He was to be obedient to His Father's will. I find it enlightening and fascinating to read the Gospels in the light of all that Jesus 'was taught by the Spirit' during those years of deep reflection in Nazareth. What did He think about? Or talk about with Mary and Joseph? What were His impressions of the neighbours, of the conversations He heard as he silently worked in the carpenter's shop? Let us look at what living in Nazareth meant for Him in the unfolding of the plan of the Godhead. Jesus was *sinless*. Sinlessness means 'goodness' continuously flowing out from Him to others, delighting many, channelling others to a new awareness, disturbing to some who could not accept a goodness which revealed their own lack; all this was a teaching through experience for Jesus. To love and to give everything was obviously not enough. His very sinlessness was a barrier between Him and sinners – or so it appeared – unless He became their **friend**! Was that what happened, so that a dominant part of His life was spent with sinners, eating with them, speaking in simple terms yet challenging in love? A lesser person would have feared for the success of His mission when He came to the Jordan to be baptised; a lesser man would have had a *private* baptism from John, who had such influence with the people; but Jesus led by the Spirit had no thought ever for Himself. He was consumed with zeal for His Father's house, with longing to establish the kingdom: 'I have come to bring fire on the earth, and how I wish it were already kindled' (Luke 12:49). This was His longing for the consummation of His mission of salvation and all of us sinners are important to Him.

Sinners: In His years in Nazareth, Jesus would have observed or heard about the way women were often oppressed by men and then treated like the woman taken in adultery . . . The scribes and Pharisees brought such a woman to Jesus 'making her stand there in full view of everybody'. Jesus knew they were setting a trap for Him. The law ordained that *both* parties to adultery be stoned, so already these men had disregarded the law.

But they persisted in their question to Jesus: 'What have you to say?' Jesus adroitly evaded the trap by refusing to give judgment, which would have meant either His violating the law or His condemning her to execution. This latter would have had the Romans upon Him as Jews were not allowed to carry out their own executions. His answer was a throwing down of the gauntlet to the accusers: 'If there is one of you who has not sinned, let him be the first to throw a stone at her' (John 8:7). He was saying that only God can judge; our role is to forgive and be compassionate; whereupon the leaders began to slip quietly away, beginning with the elders – who apparently were more aware of their sins than the younger ones!

Compassion towards sinners is a special hallmark of Jesus. It keeps recurring. The woman in the house of Simon the Pharisee experienced both His compassion and His defence of her; He was accused by His enemies of being the friend of publicans and sinners; sinners were His table companions. He had His own approach also to tax collectors who were among the most unpopular people in Israel; although Jews by birth, they chose to work for Rome – with its secular government and pagan gods – so they were considered traitors. Jesus saw deeper than other people; He won through to many sinners because *He loved them for themselves*, and His judgment was both just and merciful. It is our good fortune that Jesus is the friend of sinners, since we too are sinners, but He had little time for hypocrites or whited sepulchres. He challenged these, but even in tongue-lashing them, He was trying in *love* to break through their defences. At the first sign of repentance, Jesus would be there for them.

Love: It is wonderful to see how often the word love or the concept of charity – meaning love – is used by Jesus or in the Gospels. He loves John the beloved disciple, Lazarus and his sisters, Mary and Martha, and the rich young man, who was so foolish and blind, and many others, but especially children. I find Christ's relationship with John the Beloved and the family at Bethany heart-warming in its deep humanity. They were 'of a kind' – with the same kind of selfless spiritual outlook and hope for the future. They were a 'gift' for Jesus. One senses that with them, Jesus didn't have to be the teacher, always exhorting them to be faithful or to be zealous for the kingdom! It is one of God's rich gifts also to people, especially in ministry, when friendship is the sound basis of their spiritual growth and maturity. Then, love is real and non-possessive; then the loving allows for space to be oneself, to discern one's own responsibilities and responses, to remain free in decisions that may at times differ from one's friend, but always with respect, love and support.

Then there is too another blessed ingredient for joyful spirituality – a place for laughter or quiet humour! I always enjoy the Emmaus scene where Jesus is encouraging the two travellers, on their way to Emmaus, to explore their hidden feelings about the Crucifixion and their loss of Jesus. To their heated statement: 'You must be the only one in Jerusalem who doesn't know the things that have been happening here in the last few days,' Jesus replies, surely with His tongue in His cheek and with deep love and understanding, hiding as best He can the smile on His lips and the light in His eyes: 'What things?' He asked, as if *He* didn't know! And do you not think that He found it delightful to see small but wealthy Zaccheus being caught out up a tree so as to see more this time than just the backs of heads – which was his normal lot? Jesus was going to give him a great boost, by dining with him (a most unpopular man) so there was surely gentle raillery in inviting him to 'come down immediately' – not only from the top of the sycamore-fig tree but more importantly, 'come down from your position of power and wealth' if you truly want to be the friend of Jesus! If we do not read Christ's gentle humour here and there in the Gospels, how can we ourselves have some fun-time with Him, relaxing and at ease in His presence?

Children: I sometimes wonder how much the fact that so many little children died to ensure that the Child-Jesus lived, may have affected his 'special' attitude to little ones. The massacre of the Holy Innocents was one evident form of violence and abuse; there are unfortunately others, as we know only too well. The abuse of the weak or defenceless is always abhorrent to Jesus. 'Whoever welcomes a little child like this in my name welcomes me. But if anyone causes one of these little ones who believe in me to sin, it would be better for him to have a large millstone hung round his neck and to be drowned in the depths of the sea' (Matt. 18:5–6).

The experience of human love is necessary for us to be able to trust God's love and to respond to it. He was really saying that our fate is desperate if our behaviour is such that it sows distrust in a child's mind so that the child fears to trust even God.

Jesus was a great teacher. He liked to illustrate the points He made by using symbols or imagery. He also had a knack of asking awkward questions at times. I love this scene as told by Mark, where Jesus (knowing

His disciples) was well aware of their embarrassing talk as they journeyed. He provokes a discussion by asking the question: 'What were you arguing about on the road?' But they kept quiet because on the way they had argued about who was the greatest. They were caught up in personal success and, sometimes, their mothers were urging them on! So 'sitting down, Jesus called the Twelve and said: "If anyone wants to be first, he must be the very last, and the servant of all"' (Mark 9:35).

This last statement speaks always loudly to me of His own presence on the mountain-top and His talks with the Father about the right way forward for Himself. He speaks with quiet authority, and then proceeds to impress the lesson on the disciples by the gentleness and humility with which He treats a little child. Welcoming children in a society where they were second-class citizens was certainly a new approach! I wonder how Judas or Peter reacted to that? 'He took a little child and had him stand among them. Taking him in his arms, He said to them: "Whoever welcomes one of these little children in my name; welcomes me; and whoever welcomes me does not welcome me but the one who sent me"' (Mark. 9:36–37).

At other times, He spoke of little children in connection with the kingdom which was so precious to Him:

> Then little children were brought to Jesus for him to place His hands on them and pray for them. But the disciples rebuked those who brought them. Jesus said: 'Let the little children come to me and do not hinder them, for the kingdom of heaven belongs to such as these.' When he had placed his hands on them, he went on from there. (Matt. 19:13–15)

Jesus was using little children to explain of course that He also meant – as later St Paul likewise explained – the necessity of putting away 'childish things' when one becomes a man. Jesus uses the occasion of the success of the seventy-two and their jubilation that demons had submitted to them in His name as another teaching about children. Having warned them not to rejoice because spirits submitted to them but rather because their names were written in heaven, Jesus full of joy through the Spirit turned spontaneously to the Father with whom He was now one: 'I praise you, Father, Lord of heaven and earth, because you have hidden these things from the wise and prudent and revealed them to little children. Yes, Father, for this was your good pleasure' (Matt. 11:25). Those who are childlike, with an open and trusting heart, are the 'children' who are able to understand the Father's teaching.

This is a powerful teaching point about the heart of a child which is the way into the kingdom of God. It is a clear statement about the right focus for His followers. Having the heart of a child implies **humility, trust, dependence on the leading of the Spirit of God**. It is the 'emptying process' for a follower of Christ which parallels His own emptying when He became a human like us.

This heart of a child, this relying on the Spirit, means also that a child of God lives by a discerning heart, discerning the will of God and carrying it out at all costs, in the power of the Holy Spirit.

Little children exemplify the teaching of Jesus on the kind of kingdom He was setting up: not a kingdom of power. His parables emphasise what is 'small' yet in God's hands becomes powerful. The kingdom is like a seed which is sown on four kinds of soil; or like a mustard seed which is so small yet becomes a tree; again the kingdom will have the seed of wheat in it yet darnel will also live side by side with the wheat – the good with the less good – until God in His own time uproots the wicked. All these parables of hidden treasure, of the pearl of great price, of the fishing net, reveal how in Nazareth Jesus was seeing and recalling ordinary little things to use later in His ministry. He Himself had the open and loving heart of a child, of the Son of God, who was learning how to express simply, through everyday sights, the deepest of truths. How often does He speak of an ear of corn, a cloud, rain, a storm, a boat, a cup of water, hunger, thirst, sand, ordinary things in the life of the people. In teaching His disciples, He is of course teaching us too. The Gospels are the storehouse where a unique photograph album of his years in Nazareth is treasured. By living the Gospel message, we learn how to let Jesus of Nazareth form our Christian lives, and continue to live within us His Incarnation today. In this way, we discover that a Christian life is intended indeed to be a 'holy and a whole' experience, and that each day can be a blessed day in our individual 'Gospel' experience.

A Chance to Reflect

(if desired)

- *A Christian life is intended to be a 'holy and whole' experience.*
- *Emptying oneself of self leaves more room for the Spirit of Christ who led Jesus of Nazareth.*

- *Building the kingdom is seeking, finding and following Christ and letting Him have space and time to mould me into His image.*
- *'Truly you are a God who hides' – the hidden life is the treasure-house of the wisdom of the Gospels.*
- *'Learn of Me for I am gentle and humble of heart.'*

A Chance to Pray

(as the Spirit guides)

Come, Lord Jesus,
Open me to the guidance of Your Spirit
and help me to listen humbly
and to obey Your voice.

Jesus, I ardently desire to have the heart of a child because such a heart delights You. I need Your help, I am slow to hear, to learn and to obey. Strengthen me, dear Jesus, and help others, who, like me, desire to know You better and to love You more sincerely and generously. Amen.

7

INCARNATION – CONTINUING IN US TODAY

(Love begetting a Love-Response)

'I live now, not I, but Christ lives in me.'

This continuing Incarnation – in our humanity – is the high point of the plan of God for our salvation. 'The Word was made flesh and dwelt among us' that we, His people, might find in His human experience the Way, the Truth and the Life to inspire us to go and do likewise.

The motivation of God's plan was love, as we saw, because love is the essence of God.

The motivation of our human response to God can only likewise be love – if it is truly to build God's kingdom.

God's gift of love, in its constancy, elicits from us a response of love from our own hearts; that as love begets love, the open genuine seeker of God soon finds within him or her a longing for more. In response to that human cry to be empowered to respond more generously, God Himself, Love itself, enters more deeply within us, within 'His Home'. 'Lord Jesus, come in glory.'

The moral fibre is strengthened, the horizon is broadened; there begins a sharing of vision. One is more committed. With this deeper commitment comes also a freedom that releases the power of the Spirit within: 'It is for freedom that Christ has set us free. Stand firm, then, and do not let yourselves be burdened again by a yoke of slavery' (Gal. 5:1).

Such a burden is whatever is 'contrary to the Spirit . . . sexual immorality, impurity and debauchery; idolatry and witchcraft; hatred, discord, jealousy, fits of rage, selfish ambition, dissensions, factions and envy; drunkenness, orgies, and the like. I warn you, as I did before, that those who live like this will not inherit the kingdom of God' (Gal. 5:17–21).

This description, given by St Paul, fits closely to our experience of the world today. Those who are committed to a response of love to God are concerned not only with reconciliation for their own wrongdoing – which is always a lack of love – but desire also to 'stand in the gap' for others so that God's love be not unrequited.

Paul's advice for such people is:

> So, I say, live by the Spirit . . . the Spirit desires what is contrary to sinful nature. The fruit of the Spirit is love, joy, peace, patience, kindness, goodness, faithfulness, gentleness and self-control . . . Those who belong to Christ Jesus have crucified the sinful nature with its passions and desires. Since we live by the Spirit, let us keep in step with the Spirit. (Gal. 5:16, 22–25)

You and I have travelled a journey of love in which God's delight was clear, it was rooted in love and confirmed in scripture. Resting with the Incarnate Word in His human experience, we had further opportunity to become aware of His delight, His love but also of the cost of love to Him.

The cost, however, faded into oblivion, as we know for example from the parable of the Prodigal Son, when a response of love caused great rejoicing in heaven and on earth.

We must never lose sight of the reality that we are all sinners. Sin has to be rejected and repented of; then 'a heart of flesh' replaces our 'heart of stone'. There is, however, an amazing thing to be noted about the power of love where God's forgiveness is concerned. It is the deepest truth of the story of the prodigal. **God's forgiving is way ahead of the sinner all the time!** God's Spirit reads the heart, sees when the sorrow is sincere, runs ahead to let the repentant one know that God's longing to be 'together again' is even greater than the longing of the returning one, because God's love is so much greater. It is the quality of a sinner's repentant love that is important in this reconciliation, much more than guilt, more than working harder, more than vain promises. **Love is always what counts**. When will we learn that truth? God's love is real. We have to ask ourselves: is ours? If it is, then *we live it*, by trusting God for strength, by listening to His Spirit guiding us from within, we put our brother and sister before ourselves. Thus we begin to develop the open, selfless, God-centred 'heart of a child' which is the way into the kingdom. There is much to be taught by God after this initial reconciliation stage, but if the heart is open and sincere, it happens at the pace of the Spirit!

Learning from people who let Christ live in them

I personally learn a lot from observing people who love, from contact with them, from watching the effect they have on others. This, after all, is what we do when we recall the Incarnation of Jesus in Nazareth – it is the same principle. We look, we learn, we are strengthened to grow and to love. I propose to share with you here some of the many people whom I have found to be eager, filled with a genuine desire to live closer to God. I could, in fact, fill a book, but I want to choose what may illustrate what I have been saying about living incarnationally today, or to put it another way letting Christ live in us. We could also see them as people with 'a living faith', or people who 'live the life of the Resurrection' – whatever conveys clearly, to you, people who are committed to God, who allow His Spirit to live in them so that the Risen Christ is free to act. Let our *desire* to live this way increase so as to delight God.

A class by herself

Maryanne is my first choice. She is the only one who gets her real name. She is with God now for forty-four years! She is in fact in a class by herself, though one or two others remind me of her.

Maryanne was, I think, a rare child of God, His sheer delight, as she was in our family. She came from an orphanage run by Religious Sisters, to help my parents with nine of us children. In spirit, she became one of the family, while yet remaining a combination of housekeeper, nurse, maid of all things. My mother was a teacher, my father a shopkeeper. Her influence on me, the youngest, whom she cared for at birth when my mother was seriously ill, remains to this day. Her memory remains as green as ever. She was tended by my mother for the last months of her life and is buried beside my parents. When in religious life we were advised to try to be a 'still-point' in life for others, I knew what was meant. That was Maryanne. Serenity marked her. She loved each of us and she was loved. 'Maryanne is a treasure' is how the extended family referred to her. But I felt I knew why . . .

She was different. As a little one, I slept with her. She was the first to awaken my creativity! Each night, like two children, we created and lived the next section in our serial: 'Mrs Brown's Cows'! The laughter was muffled but hilarious. Then, I clearly remember – and Maryanne could be quietly firm – she would say: 'Before we sleep, let us thank the good God for laughter, and joy and for all the blessings of this day on this home. May we sleep well, and in the morning waken to do His holy will for another day.'

By 5.30 next morning, if it were summer time, Maryanne was up to enjoy her morning swim in the sea-inlet which was a twenty-minute walk away. Later in life, she told me that there she had God and the sea all to herself! After that, she was ready, she said, for whatever the new day brought. Surely wisdom, taught only by God.

Two last memories. As we all knelt for the family rosary in the evenings, I knew instinctively that Maryanne was not then available to me. She was in her stillness. If we younger people were restless, a gentle but firm hand rested on our heads. Somehow it was enough. This was Maryanne's time. When she was dying, all that I believed about her became clear to me. The red tape to get me home to see her was finally cut. Her doctor said she should have died days ago but that she was waiting for me to come home. As I entered her room, I can still see the face filled with pain but lit with love when she saw me. Then she said, weakly but firmly: 'I want you to say the rosary with me. Then, promise me that you will leave immediately. I can now go to God.' My heart was breaking but I did as she said. My mother told me later that Maryanne waited until she heard the hall door bang. Then she went home to God.

Maryanne's gift of loving was paramount; from it flowed her fidelity to our family and to her duties. Her love extended even to her chickens and goslings; her vegetables. Almighty God was always for her 'the Good God', the Father who loved her as did His Son. I owe very much to my dear parents – love, opportunity, good example, wisdom – but Maryanne touched my deepest inner core in a way that was somehow a 'knowing God'. A simple life, like Nazareth. A simple child of God, yet of all those I know she was the closest to God. As I said – His sheer delight.

Some of God's other children

The majority of others whom I know seem to travel somewhere in the middle: people who long to be brought closer to God but are humbly aware of the necessity of much inner cleansing. Then the focus is fixed on God and this is His delight. I find that such people are held back from even closer intimacy by reason of a clinging to something, whatever that may be. It can be a *fear* to let go – lest control slips from them. Only God's love can release from that bondage. In the meantime, they live the life of the Resurrection, as we all must do, because without God we cannot even say 'Abba, Father'. Fidelity to the struggle, holding on despite problems, wins God's heart. They are very precious people, whom He calls to trust Him more; His love will always surround them. Without even knowing it, they are allowing God to live in them. They are living incarnationally, even at this stage, but they will come closer still once they let go wholeheartedly to God.

One such was *Dan* – not his real name. A good man, but at first not exactly Gospel-greedy! He enjoyed high living. A caring friend was used by God to introduce him to a parish mission and weekly prayer-life meetings. It was the right time, God's time for Dan. He took it seriously; he committed himself to daily prayer and to letting that change his life. He became more caring for others, more approachable. Becoming redundant had been instrumental in the first steps of this transformation. Eventually, he responded to the offer of a good job in his line abroad. He went, took his 'spiritual book that had opened his eyes and heart' with him; was very successful, well liked; in six months he fell off his horse and was dead before he touched ground.

At his funeral, people talked: his older brothers and sisters were curious to know what Dan had been up to which had changed him so much. Instead of the stranger he had once become, they had discovered again his love, his concern, his interest in them and an ability to talk easily about God. In and through this transformation and death, he witnessed to God's power as he had never expected to be able to do. Truly our God is a God of love and of surprises!

Colin had struggled for years with his poor self-image, with his jealousy and envy of others who outshone him, where he felt he just plodded. He was a pessimist rather than an optimist. He cared deeply for his family yet found it difficult to communicate with them.

Despite all this, his *fidelity* to prayer, his honesty in trying to know the truth about himself, his constant struggle with pride – refusing to hide behind a pseudo-humility front – continually amazed me. He gave of his utmost to God and to others at all times. I know he suffered but he usually did not use that to make a bid for sympathy. No matter what happened, he was faithful to daily prayer, to discernment, to facing the truth about himself. He has gradually come to believe that God loves him, though often it is very hard going. I believe that his manliness in hanging in there, in helping others despite how he feels, is his way of loving God. I believe that God honours that and is delighted at such fidelity when many of us would have thrown it all in. Colin's experience keeps reminding me that each of us is different; God's plan for each is between Him and the person; there will be many surprises when we all meet one day at the Throne. Only Almighty God knows, and in His wisdom and vision carries often close to the heart those who do not appear to shine. He Himself is the light and the lamp to encourage us where the way is rough. Fidelity is the watchword:

> As your word unfolds, it gives light
> and the simple understand. (Ps. 119:130)

Led by the Spirit

My special gratitude to God has been that through a third special group of His Body, He continually teaches me. I am blessed in knowing many of these who are 'led by the Spirit', who live by that Spirit and have become themselves free spirits: people who are either deeply in love with Almighty God or are on what seems to be the final break-through experience.

In a strange way, these seem to have a lot in common, though their life-experience is vastly different.

Common factors are that in their freedom of spirit they don't waste time unduly on analysing themselves or where they are with God or ought they to do more, or . . . that is all behind them. As very busy people, they learnt that unless God builds the house, all is in vain. According to who they are, this becomes a priority. Their spirituality is fully God-centred, neighbour-centred. Even in family matters, they are free – or work towards it. They put family first, but not taking up all their energy and interest. They truly love their children dearly, but in a non-possessive way and with a strong dose of common sense. They see the trap in trying to take on too much responsibility – a subtle form of running people's lives! All share ministry of one kind or another. Having freely received, they desire to give freely. Some have learnt the hard way that we can all be done without. This brings the wisdom to see that nobody is indispensable and that each of us needs space, refreshment and renewal. Otherwise we go stale. We dare not lose the gift of wonder and of expecting surprises from God:

> See, I am doing a new deed
> even now it comes to light;
> can you not see it? (Isa. 43:19)

They ensure – each in his or her own way – that they have frequent **faith-sharing**. This binds them together as the Body of Christ; it ensures honesty; it is a reliable channel of truth, since as free people seeking God who is Truth, they recognise the gift of honest feedback.

They are marked by courage, generosity and selflessness. Many have experienced great vulnerability. Their creativity keeps being renewed in a variety of ways;

their tendency – which surely is God's delight – is to seek, whenever possible in ministry, the less-advantaged. When nerves get raw, or pressure is too great, there are loving companions at hand, who spell it out in love, and help is assured before any damage can be done to themselves or to those to whom they minister.

In these examples of people who live in the power of the Spirit, we see that living incarnationally, or living the life of Resurrection, takes place in simple ways, in ordinary daily living. It is all the work of God.

This is all a rich experience of 'church together'. It is usually ecumenical. The signs of the Spirit cited before (Gal. 5:22–26) are confirmatory. Yet the enemy is always on the prowl, seeking whom he can devour. Sharing their own reality, praying together, discerning the various spirits is a blessed gift and a healing one: 'If God is for us, who can be against us?' Humility is greatly desired and prayed for by these seekers of closeness to God: 'Learn of me, for I am gentle and humble of heart' (Matt. 11:29). Such a prayer is always answered because humility is very dear to Christ who lives within us.

Some of these have been greatly helped by the experience of a desert retreat, where one seeks God alone – not His gifts. We believe that the simpler our approach to God, the better. The journey, however, is always a challenge. No matter how close God is, we ourselves remain an uncertain factor! I share in a later chapter what has helped many of us in desert retreats. May you too be blessed!

A Chance to Reflect

YOU
are to be
taken
blessed
broken
distributed
that the work
of the
INCARNATION
may go
forward

St Augustine

A Chance to Pray

You have made us for Yourself, O Lord,
and our hearts are restless until they rest in You.
St Augustine

Jesus, my lack of silence makes me more restless than ever. The noise of my life does not help me either. I am hiding from You in the excessive noise. You say: 'Be still and know that I am God.' How true that is. I know it. Banish any fear I have of silence! Teach me to discover its richness and its fullness. You fill it, Lord! You are the richness in silence.

ENRICHING HELPS

Deepening the Love-Experience

8

THE HOLY SPIRIT

The God who loves us and accompanies us every step of the journey is infinitely generous in the help that He gives us. Our delight in coming a little closer to Him is nothing compared with His delight in our letting Him lead us and transform us. He knows – and we know by this time – that increasing nearness to Him opens us to being more involved with our sisters and brothers. It also means that closeness and fidelity mean a deeper sharing of His vision. That we frequently fail is a sadness for us but no longer a calamity, if we have learnt a lesson that will heal us. Formerly we owned our faults, and desired forgiveness, but greater closeness now means our sorrowing, not so much because we have failed again, but because we rejected His love and His help. We could have been better used by Him in spreading His kingdom had our self-love not obtruded so much.

All of this is profitable learning on the journey. One of the greatest helps is the certainty that scripture is being fulfilled: 'All shall be taught by God.' This teaching may come through other people, the members of Christ's Body; it may come through prayerful reflection on an experience, through reading, through various forms of human communication; but always the *saving action* comes in and through the Holy Spirit.

The greatest help in our daily, everyday activities, in every breath, thought or action flows from the Holy Spirit. Every good desire we have is a gift from above – from the Holy Spirit. All good that is achieved in and through us is essentially the work of the Holy Spirit. It will indeed be a tremendous help to us, if on our journey of love we come to recognise and be familiar with the movements of the Holy Spirit, who *is* love.

Elsewhere I have written about the Holy Spirit.[1] Here, however, I want to give practical help in getting to know the *power* of the Spirit.

Desire to grow in awareness of the Spirit's action and to be led by the Spirit, I found, was a beginning for me in my early days. I followed that up with reading about the Holy Spirit in a simple theology book suitable for beginners. Better knowledge about the Spirit increased my desire to know Him better.

That led me to scripture. The Acts of the Apostles made the Holy Spirit more real, more a part of the Church. I remember reading at one time that by faith, any believer can claim the Holy Spirit's power to do Christ's work. Someone else told me that the Holy Spirit gives us the motivation, energy, courage and ability to spread the word of God. I began to experience – in small ways – the truth of this and the power to attempt it. I read or heard that wherever real love is found, there is the action of the Holy Spirit. All of this I found exciting, stimulating and challenging to experience for myself.

At that time, over fifty years ago, I hadn't *clearly* grasped that where Jesus is, there is the Spirit. A day came when I began reading Romans and came to what is now one of my favourite passages in scripture, which I give here in full. It seemed almost too, too good to be true. I felt I must be misunderstanding. St Paul had been talking about 'hope'. Then he went on:

> In the same way, the Spirit helps us in our weakness. We do not know what we ought to pray for, but the Spirit himself intercedes for us with groans that words cannot express. And he who searches our hearts knows the mind of the Spirit, because the Spirit intercedes for the saints in accordance with God's will.
>
> (Rom. 8:26–27)

For a long time, that passage nourished me and I began to depend greatly on the Holy Spirit. In the early 1950s, teaching on the inner life dealt more with grace versus sin; to me as a child that teaching was connected with a 'shining interior quality' which left me quite cold! Foolishly and erroneously, I associated 'sin' with ugly, black spots on my soul, while 'grace' conjured up in my imagination a shining sheath. I found neither life nor love in that false imagery of grace. At the time, I was lonely and lost. A good friend, a Religious Sister, with whom I could talk about God and my longing to know Him better, had been transferred to one of our communities in the United States; it seemed to mean separation for ever. The human contact had greatly helped me in my spiritual search; now it was gone and human problems with an authority figure were looming on the horizon. It seemed to me that neither God nor humans were any longer on my side. Yet, somehow, I really knew God was there.

I was sitting on a seat in the garden on a beautiful

morning in summer. School was closed. Chores were complete; there was a short space to think or to be. I loved our particular convent church. To me it had an atmosphere of prayer rarely found anywhere else. I used to feel that many holy women had prayed there and blessed the place. It was a hallowed spot. I was enjoying the peace of the garden, and was silently calling on God to help me, to send me light and understanding. Very gently, I began to recognise a change in my being. *My spirits lifted unaccountably*. Though I was looking towards the church, my awareness became centred on my 'inner being'. For the first time, I began to understand the reality that each of us is truly a temple of the Holy Spirit; I seemed to experience the Spirit as *a living presence within me.* I was no longer left 'cold' as my misunderstanding of grace had left me. I felt there was something I had to do, but not just yet. Now I just had to let the Spirit within me rejoice and take care of me . . . I had only to rest in Him.

This happened on a Thursday, a day on which we spent an hour in the church before Jesus in the Tabernacle to commemorate the Last Supper and all He had done for us. I began from that day of 'my garden experience' to dedicate every Thursday to the Holy Spirit; it became a very special day. I used to waken with joy; nothing could upset me on a Thursday, it became grist to the mill of His presence and His care. Eventually I shared with another Sister what had happened and how important Thursdays were for me. I was afraid she would not believe me. But she joined me in making Thursdays her way too of discovering God's presence alive within her. I felt supported in human as well as in divine terms. Jesus and the Holy Spirit were no longer 'separate'. I grasped that the Holy Spirit was the mutual love of the Father and the Son, and that the Holy Spirit was the Spirit of the Risen Jesus. All was well! Each of us is the temple of the Holy Spirit.

When the Holy Spirit began to be present in ordinary, little, everyday things (not just Thursdays), I began to discover the importance of *discernment* as a way of living in the Spirit. By this time, I had begun to talk to groups about the Spirit, to encourage others to be led by Him. I gradually understood that not just the Spirit but the Trinity is at home within us, as Jesus promised in the Last Discourse (John 14:10–21).

Discernment

I do not wish to repeat here what I have written before in *Light Out of Darkness* about discernment.[2] I wish to be practical about the gift of discernment. What is it? It is a gift of the Spirit. It is *a recognition* that too often we tend to live with and in unreality – that is the absence of truth! This can happen when we are not in touch with our *real* selves nor with the movements of the Spirit. Consequently, we cover up, we see situations as we would like them to be, not as they actually are. This is folly and is disruptive of human relationships, not to mention our relationship with God.

Discernment is a gift of the Spirit. In a dream, God said to Solomon: 'Ask for whatever you want me to give you.' Solomon answered: '. . . Give your servant a discerning heart to govern your people and to distinguish between right and wrong.' . . . The Lord was pleased [and said] . . . 'I will do what you have asked. I will give you a wise and discerning heart . . .' [Thus] God gave Solomon wisdom and very great insight, and a breadth of understanding as measureless as the sand on the seashore' (1 Kgs. 3:5, 9, 12; 4:29).

We cannot walk in the way of the Lord, being taught by God, unless we have the gift of discernment and try to use it always. We must therefore pray for it – with words, yes, but especially by what we call 'the prayer of the heart'. This is the prayer of stillness, where we are present to God, where we stay close to Him, holding nothing back; where we let make-believe go and speak *our utter need and truth to God* – with faith and hope and love. Having poured out our truth to Him, we listen, heart to heart. We do not hear words – God speaks at a deeper level; when we are in tune with God's way, God's will, then **He speaks through peace of heart**, even when thorns may still press. God does not promise to remove all obstacles so that we may enjoy an easy journey to Him. He promises to remove all obstacles to our closeness, if He finds we are ready. Discernment means then that we are trusting God, that we are truly listening, and that we are willing to hear and obey. Never will He let us be led astray when our relationship is that of trust. If, however, we are being misled by the wily enemy, we will not experience true peace and contentment; hopefully, we may experience unease and an awareness that all is not well. Then we pray for light and strength; at times, if we are in darkness and are being misled, then we may receive the gift of light, or such a sense of unease that we cannot rest. We must cry out for God's help: 'Lord, that I may see and may follow You.'

Discernment can be experienced – if we will – every day, in the work-place, in the street, at home, in prayer, *literally everywhere*. The truth is that God knows we must discern what is His will, otherwise we are following our own way like blind people. As we use this gift and bless and thank God for it, we become more expert in discovering His will. We may not be able to follow easily or totally what we discover, but then we know what we can do: we pray deeply within our being, where the Spirit is in the temple that we are; we remind the Spirit of our weakness and that Jesus has given Him to us to strengthen us and enlighten us. Then we become still, focused on God within us, waiting and, at times, praising, thanking and glorifying Him for all that He is doing for us.

To become sensitive to the movements of God within us is a great help on this journey of love. Often we can be taken quite by surprise; and sometimes such a surprise-gift changes our lives. This can happen when God wishes to turn our lives upside down, so that we 'let go' more easily and let God become the centre of our lives. It is all part of the gift of discernment, and is a gift of love and new life for us.

It happened to me in this way. About ten years ago, I was deep into ministry yet 'something' kept nudging me. You may ask: 'So what more did you want?' My answer now with hindsight would be: '*I* didn't know I was looking for more, but *God* knew I *needed* more.' That's a big difference! I was on a team giving a weekend on some spiritual themes.[3] It was going very well. I was very grateful. Then I was surprised when, just after lunch, I felt a pressing, indeed an urgent need, to have my team-colleagues pray for me! I felt embarrassed! Time was limited and it could have appeared to be a very selfish, self-centred need, especially as I didn't even know what I wanted, still less what God seemed to be saying! I felt very foolish indeed. Nevertheless, I was convinced that God had a reason which I could not understand but must obey! The team prayed and we handed the situation over to God – without receiving any greater clarity! I could only trust God and accept the situation. Then a friend said to me: 'That is the first time in all the years I have known you that I saw you vulnerable.' I was struck dumb; it felt like an unintentional put-down! *God speaks in strange ways at times.* I did not know at that time that God had just spoken the first word to me of a new conversion experience through the remark of my friend! My hurt response was: 'And what have I been doing all weekend but revealing my vulnerability?!' 'Ah no,' he said, 'Through your own sharing, you have beautifully revealed God's goodness to all of us when we are vulnerable. But you yourself had already come through the pain to a good place.' 'Go now,' he continued, 'and tell the group how vulnerable you *actually are right now.*' I gasped!

Vulnerability

I seemed struck by lightning. This was a whole new scene. My friend's insight was right and I recognised that. But how could I expose my present vulnerability to people whom I had been helping through those days? How could I say that I had asked my colleagues to pray with me, because suddenly I had felt lost, didn't know why I felt God was nudging me, leaving me restless and uncertain? Then I recognised how we can rationalise anything, wipe it out as of no account, when we don't want to do it. My struggle to be open and honest was truly a fierce one. I very nearly didn't make it, but my loyal friends were praying for me and with me.

My claiming a vulnerability that I myself didn't even

understand was, as was later declared by the group, the greatest gift I had given that weekend to the participants. As for myself, only God knows what I would have missed if I hadn't got out of the seat of control and let my brokenness surface. The Spirit's action in letting me discover my vulnerability at a depth hitherto unrecognised by me achieved more for my growth in a short time than I could have done in a lifetime. I have learnt to value highly the wisdom that is hidden in our acknowledging our vulnerability. Vulnerability is, I think, a gift God gives us to help us become more *prudent*. I had to learn that. I would now go so far as to say that knowing and acknowledging one's vulnerability – at least to oneself – is the beginning of **a new growth in wisdom**. Without it, we are in danger of thinking that we have everything under control, that we ourselves are totally 'together'. This can be a great blindness on our part. If we are growing as Christians, then necessarily we are *changing*; so to change means walking a new way, with a new rhythm, perhaps with untried instruments. This exposes us to some uncertainty, to surprises, perhaps to the possibility of being hurt or wounded. This is our vulnerability. We risk being vulnerable for the sake of the new growth. Being vulnerable teaches us a little humility. Discernment helps greatly.

A discerning heart is one of God's greatest helps on our journeying with Him into love.

The hidden value in diminishments

Diminishments can occasion groans! All kinds of diminishments are a form of vulnerability which, as we have seen, can result in a blessing. Vulnerability literally means 'able to be wounded'. Jesus Christ was very vulnerable – and 'by His wounds we are saved'. So too our vulnerability can be used by God to bring light to ourselves or to others. Vulnerability is a form of suffering!

I do not know any answer to the mystery of suffering except that, in some strange way, it helps to get us out of the seat of control, out of having status and power, of having it all together.

Vulnerability goes against everything that, as humans, we work for and are urged in our society to attain, for example to get on top, to be in control, to have it good, to succeed. When diminishments make us vulnerable, it can seem at first as if life is at an end and all is a cruel joke. The truth is that the more we are on top, having the world at our feet, the more crushing seemingly are the diminishments. *Yet that is not the whole story.* The more we are on top (if we are truly on top with God), praising Him for what life, with its ups and downs, has made of us, that gives us a new kind of energy to cope differently with diminishments, with other forms of vulnerability, even with suffering. If we keep the focus on God, then the very diminishments which upset us initially prove to be a much richer gift than any we had before. The gift is the valuable experience of **losing one's life so as to gain it**; it is dying so that another can rise; it is the grain of wheat dying so that there will be a rich harvest which many can enjoy.

Of course, the Spirit has to support one through all this, as it goes contrary to human nature. One has to be taught a new approach to a new experience, but it works! In listening to the Spirit, one learns the way to handle it as Jesus taught us. It is, in fact, not a way, it is an *attitude*, an attitude of surrender and joy! It is, nevertheless, a painful process; it can be humiliating; one can be treated like an infant although one's intellect is fully alive; at times, one thinks one can almost smell death; depression seems to lurk around the corner, if not already a new companion.

Nor is it only the elderly who experience some form of diminishment which makes people vulnerable. **Redundancy** is a major cause of this experience; **unemployment**, especially for the young who have never had the thrill of their first job, their first wage-packet; **lack of success** with the peer group; not being a success in making 'dates'; being insufficiently loved at home, in school, at play, having been traumatised, in any way, as a child, is a form of diminishment.

I am definitely *not* saying that the first step in these situations is to lead those who are suffering into an awareness of the Holy Spirit, in the spiritual sense! I do say again, however, that where there is true human love, **there is the Holy Spirit of God in action**.

Human support, when it is genuine loving support, is a necessary base for opening one to the support of the Spirit. The wisdom in human support *is* the presence of the Holy Spirit in it. A believer can therefore add this awareness to his or her ministry to the enrichment of others. Nevertheless, God's love reaches all His children, believers or non-believers, in ways beyond our understanding.

I stress therefore **human support as a God-given gift**, without which one cannot grow, cannot even understand God's love. So often, human loving is the *first* way – as in the case of a child – that God's love becomes possible and real for others. On that sure foundation of human love, the way forward is through the power of the Holy Spirit.

In my own case, I had the experience of many years of access to the Holy Spirit. Nevertheless, it was the loving, wise, human support of Eilish, my friend, which lately released in me the power of the Spirit *at a new depth*. This is why I say with conviction that a friend, who lives in Christ, accustomed to discerning, becomes His life-giving presence for another when only God can suffice. Throughout my latest experience of diminishment – inner-ear problems which were like a dying, a loss of control – I still knew that God alone was what I desired. I had to claim that truth. Yet, parallel with that was the reality of powerlessness, a loss, a deprivation of giftedness which had been customary. I had been confirmed frequently as having the gift of perceptivity, not only in ministry for others but also in a clarity of awareness of my own inner life. Now, nothing at all was clear! Nothing. I *felt* like a zombie, yet I didn't act like one. I surrendered to the 'present moment', to whatever that involved, but without any sense of certainty or clarity. It was only when new life was given to me in the Holy Land and I came out of the tomb like Lazarus, that lost energy and life were restored. It was when I was renewed that my friend, Eilish, shared how she had experienced me in my vulnerability and powerlessness. She says that that experience of mine strengthened her and she assures me it can help others too. All of this was unknown to me at the time; it was not of my doing or volition and therefore it could only have been the work of the Spirit – 'when we are too weak even to pray for ourselves, the Spirit does it for us' (Rom. 8:26–27). I rejoice therefore to reveal His strength in the weakness of vulnerability.

Eilish said that she experienced me, for the first time

ever, as beginning to be my age! She saw the pain and the cost of my powerlessness, and she shared it in her own heart. At each new experience of diminishment – especially increasing deafness – she says that she saw and heard my ongoing acceptance of what was happening by my continuous handing over to God the pain of each present moment. I can honestly say this was truly *not* part of my awareness, beyond my trusting the Spirit to take all and use all for God's glory. I had no deep inner experience, except surrender, at all. My friend added that, for her, in observing the power of the Spirit at work, she was able to let go her own fear of diminishment. She now knows that, in the power of the Spirit, diminishments can become an experience of being found in God; not just an experience of enduring or of accepting, but an experience of allowing the Spirit to be with a person, in and through the diminishments, so that they become blessed, holy with His presence, and therefore life-giving for others. The zombie that I was knew only that I was clinging to the Spirit! The rest was His healing work. Praise be to Almighty God.

The Holy Spirit's role of Sanctifier in our lives is so very vital that I would like to tabulate the main thoughts in the above, in the hope that some may be helped and renewed as I have been through *powerlessness*.

- *Let us greatly desire to know the Holy Spirit intimately.*
- *Let us pray frequently that God will give us the grace to live by the Holy Spirit's power, by reflecting on Romans 8:26–27 and by trying to leave the Spirit space in our hearts and lives to act on our behalf.*
- *Let us read scripture which refers to the Holy Spirit,*

ponder its meaning for our lives, and put it into practice.

- *Let us say the 'Glory be to the Father, and to the Son, and to the Holy Spirit . . .' frequently, to honour the Trinity present within us.*
- *Let us pause a few times each day to recall the presence of the Spirit within us and to beg His guidance in this moment or in this dilemma.*
- *Let us be guided by the Spirit in our attitude to all diminishments.*
- *Let us give praise, glory and thanks to Almighty God for the gift of the Holy Spirit.*

A Chance to Reflect

For this reason, I bow my knees before the Father, from whom every family in heaven and on earth is named, that according to the riches of His glory He may grant you to be strengthened with might through His Spirit in the inner man, and that Christ may dwell in your hearts through faith; that you, being rooted and grounded in love, may have power to comprehend with all the saints what is the breadth and length and height and depth, and to know the love of Christ which surpasses knowledge, that you may be filled with all the fullness of God.

(Eph. 3:14–19)

A Chance to Pray

Jesus answered him, 'If a man loves me, he will keep my word,
and my Father will love him,
and we will come to him and make our home with him.
But the Counsellor, the Holy Spirit,

whom the Father will send in my name, will teach you all things,
and bring to your remembrance all that I have said to you.
Peace I leave with you; my peace I give to you;
not as the world gives do I give to you.
Let not your hearts be troubled, neither let them be afraid.
(John 14:23, 26, 27)

Lord, let our prayers rise like incense before You.

Holy spirit, fill me with Your Life, Your presence,
Your wisdom and Your strength.
When I am weak, let me fly to our strength which
covers me and delights my God! You are Love –
teach me to love You each day, more and more.

9

PRAYER

Prayer with a Difference

I will not repeat here what has been published before.[1] However, I would like to take a practical look at prayer which fits in both with the role of the Holy Spirit and with the general thrust of this book: *understanding Incarnation so that we let Christ live it within us today.*

I wish to broaden the whole concept of prayer, so that it differs little from the daily action of the Holy Spirit in and through little events and the life in Christ which we are called to live: 'I live now, not I but Christ lives in me' (Gal. 2:20). As always however, it is wise first to ensure that the basics, the sure foundation, are firmly in place.

Prayer is our relationship with God rooted in the reality of who God is and who we are. As sinners, therefore, relating to Almighty God, our Saviour, who loves us infinitely, we recognise the privilege it is to be able to address God, to be able to know Him and trust Him, to be able, in the Spirit, to respond to His love with the love and adoration of our hearts.

Prayer is one of the ways in which God teaches us all that we need to know.

PRAYER

Prayer is our opportunity to listen to God, to speak to Him, to sit with Him, to be led into different kinds of relationship with Him.

Through prayer, God helps us to see where our lives need to change so that we grow into the image and likeness of God. This 'behaviour change' affects the way we respond every moment, to different people, to different situations, to different stimuli or nudges from the Spirit of God. It is the way we discern what God calls us to do or to avoid.

Through listening to God in prayer, we are taught to discern when God is moving us from one type of prayer to another. It may be a temporary change of prayer-style to help us let go, not become over-attached to what is familiar, to let us discover new ways, new approaches, learn new lessons, become more rooted in one or other gift, as humility, love, silence, stillness . . . We learn that it is not the particular form of prayer that is so important but how it helps or prevents us from focusing on God Himself rather than ourselves.

Fidelity to prayer is essential. Spasmodic orgies in prayer are usually pretty useless and result more from self-interest, motivated by the onslaught of fear, anxiety, a self-centred desire to excel, subverted pride at our non-progress, or even a frontal attack on God to ensure that He recognises our wonderful selves! There is need here to discern the spirits! The darkness involved needs to be redeemed by God who is Light.

Fidelity to prayer brings a recognition that we are sinners, are therefore given to prefer the easy route, the bright and sparkling way, rather than the steady, consistent daily prayer period which is our commitment of good intent and love. It is this fidelity which ensures the solid foundation that releases the power of the Spirit to test our fledgling wings in new areas.

It is this fidelity which familiarises us with the movements of the Spirit within us – the movements which either attract us to God or movements which alert us to a danger zone where the enemy lurks to catch the lovers of self. Through discernment, we really come to know the Spirit. We come to be delicately sensitive to His presence and to the gentle firmness and clarity of His approach. He speaks and moves clearly. The choice to listen to Him and to follow is always ours. The Holy Spirit is courtesy itself!

Before leaving these basic yet sound ways of prayer, I want to make a point. When someone complains about not being able to pray, about distractions, about interruptions, the following is what I want to say, showing the connection between building a human relationship and building a friendship of love with God:

- *Prayer* is our effort to form and develop a relationship of love with God.
- Let us learn from forming and developing human relationships: are *both* parties serious about this relationship or is one of them inclined to dabble in it, while waiting for a more appealing relationship elsewhere? Without genuine desire on both sides, there is no future in such a relationship. (God is always totally committed, so we have only to check out our side of the situation.)
- Supposing both parties are committed to a certain human relationship. There still remain some possible pitfalls: Are they eager and willing to give time to one another – not being spasmodic about

it? Are they willing to try to be totally honest with one another – no playing games, no make-believe, no childish immaturity? When a problem arises, do they face that together, or is it brushed under the carpet? In short, are there no-go areas between them? Is there any unwillingness to face reality both as an individual and together? This honesty is central to all good relationships. Dishonesty here means that this couple will talk about anything and everything except the misunderstanding of the present moment. *That is the dying point of the relationship.* Any negative attitude means lack of trust, immaturity, an unwillingness to learn and to risk together.

What is true for a human relationship like this is true in every detail about prayer. My observation after many years of pastoral ministry is that prayer cannot get off the ground seriously where there is no commitment, little real desire and less effort. Likewise, without being present to one another (which is what silence and stillness are all about) there is no life. Even when these factors are present, too often – for a variety of reasons – the pray-er will begin to pray anywhere except where his or her main interest is; if there is a problem, they seem to shove that under the carpet and begin by trying to praise God! The greatest praise of God is to talk to Him in our own language, to say how glad we are to be able to come and share with Him what is killing us and continue from there, maybe in tears, maybe in anger or near-despair, but it is real and it is sharing our truth and reality with our God who loves us and longs to hold us close.

God is even more interested in the development of

our prayer-life than we are, but we must co-operate, as we can clearly see from the human situation cited above. We are the same person whether we find ourselves in a human or in a spiritual situation, whether we are dealing with what we would call 'mundane' matters or directly with God. The advantage for us believers is that we believe God is present with us in *both* situations, but we leave Him out of both too often and for different reasons!

We leave Him out of the *human* situation from the half-conscious thought that Almighty God should be in our front room not in our basement. He is left out of the *spiritual* situation sometimes for the same reason – as if God should be treated in a more up-market way. At other times, He is left out of the heart of the spiritual situation because *we* are running the show. We're sparing God a lot of trouble and besides, we like control and God can be pretty slow at times. Our pace has definitely an edge on the Holy Spirit!

Vocal prayers

If vocal prayers are rattled off, they don't do a lot of good, not even if they are the psalms from the Divine Office. That at least is my experience. I prefer in certain circumstances to read one stanza of a psalm slowly, with the Spirit praying it with me, than to try to read the whole Office prayer – just to 'get it done'.

Vocal prayers can be downgraded – to our great loss. If I'm listening to the Spirit within me even during vocal prayer, I can recognise and discern what line or phrase helps me to come closer to God, and to my neighbour. What helps me today may not be the same for tomorrow. But the Spirit is always available, always eager to guide and to lead us. We can trust Him and He never falls asleep!

'Our Father'

If we were to join the Twelve as they ask Jesus to teach them how to pray the 'Our Father', where would our *eyes* and *ears* and *heart* be? Try that kind of prayer and see what you get from it. Ask Jesus if it pleased Him. Thank Him for teaching you, no matter what the outcome was for you. If you did not get much from it, don't sweep that reality under the carpet. Talk to Jesus about it, let your heart be in your words and thus you are combining *vocal prayer* with a simple *prayer of the heart*.

Another way to pray the 'Our Father' is to recall the promise of Jesus in the Cenacle Room after the Last Supper. There He promised that He Himself would pray for us (John 17:20). We have a choice here. We'll begin with your sitting at the feet of Jesus who has told you how much He loves His Father – and you. Then, with His Hand on your head, listen to Him with *the ears of your heart* as He prays that prayer – to His Father – with you in mind. Reflect on that experience and maybe you will want to try it some other time, so as to deepen the experience. Or perhaps you could try this – Jesus delights when we join Him in saying a 'Yes' to His Father with Him. Scripture says: 'The Son of God, the Christ Jesus, that we proclaimed among you was never "yes" and "no"; with Him it was always "yes", and however many the promises God made, the "yes" to them all is in him (Christ Jesus). That is why it is "through him" that we answer Amen to the praise of God' (2 Cor. 1:19–20).

So let us either **let Jesus pray** the 'Our Father' within us and like a refrain, we keep saying 'yes' to every bit of it with Him, or **let Jesus hold us** close, delighting Himself in our efforts to pray as He prays, focused on the Father, while His eyes bless us throughout. The important thing is to keep communicating with Jesus, who is delighting in teaching us.

The 'Our Father' is just one vocal prayer, but how rich it is when we try to pray with Jesus or through the Spirit.

We cannot leave the 'Our Father' prayer without praying also Charles de Foucauld's prayer of abandonment to the Father. This is not an easy prayer to pray and to be sincere about the sentiments expressed. You may find that you can only pray a line or two. Try to 'read' it all, however, and know that this prayer has sanctified many people. By reading it all, but not taking it all on board for yourselves, you become aware of its depth. See what speaks to you at this moment, as you read, and talk to God about that. Leave for another time, or indeed for much later, what you find at the moment is not yet for you. Praise and thank God for the gift of prayer.

FATHER, I abandon myself
into Your hands;
Do with me what You will.
Whatever You may do, I thank You.
I am ready for all, I accept all; let only
Your will be done in me
and in all Your creatures
I wish no more than this, O Lord.
Into Your hands I commend my spirit;
I offer it to You with all the love of my heart.
For I love You, Lord, and so need to give,
to surrender myself into Your hands

without reserve, and with confidence
beyond all questioning.
Because You are my Father.

Another great favourite is the prayer *'Love me as you are'*. This has helped many people to return to God or to come closer to Him. It speaks for itself. Take it slowly and, as with all prayers or 'words of God', they reveal more truth and hope and love, the oftener we pray them and listen to God.

I know your misery, the inner struggle of your heart. I also know the weaknesses of your heart. I am aware of your cowardice, your sins and your falls. I still tell you 'Love me as you are'. If you wait to be an angel before you give me your love, you will never love me. Even if you often fall again into sins you are ashamed of, even if you are poor in the practice of virtue, I do not allow you not to love me. Love me as you are! Yes, give me your heart at all times and in whatever dispositions you may be, in fervour or in dryness, faithful or unfaithful, love me as you are.

I want the love of your poor heart. If you want to be perfect before giving me your heart, you will never love me. What can prevent me from turning every grain of sand into a shining radiant archangel of great nobility? Don't you believe that I could bring into being thousands of saints, more perfect and loving than those I have created? Am I not the Almighty God? But if I choose to be loved, here and now, by your limited heart in preference to more perfect love . . . will you refuse . . . can you refuse?

Allow me to love you, my dear child. I long to win your heart. Oh, yes, I do want to mould you to better things, but in the meantime I love you as you are. I only wish you could do the same! I desire the very kind of love you can give me; the love that comes up from the bottom of your misery, because I truly love you in your very weakness, I treasure the love of the poor, the love of the weak that cries without sound: 'Lord, I love you.' It is this cry that comes from the bottom of your hearts, that matters to me, because this is real.

I don't need your achievements, your gifts, your virtues. I have not laid down high goals for you. I created you for the purpose of loving, of loving me, and not that you become puffed-up and self-centred. When you are centred on loving me as you are, then you free me to do great things for you. In this present moment, therefore, in these circumstances, just love me! Then I will achieve in you more than you could ever have dreamed.

Today, I, the Lord of Lords, stand at the door of your heart as a beggar. I knock and I wait. Do hurry to open, my heart is eager, do not make your misery an excuse. Your misery is my excuse for loving you more! Yes, you are poor and weak, even more than you know. But I know it, and I love you all the more with tender compassion. Believe me, trust me, love me. This is all I ask. I will do the rest.

I want you to think of me during the day as often as you can. I want you to think of me as a friend, as one on whom you can rely, who will never let you down. Will you do that for me as a way to love me as you are? I want you to act out of love, no matter how small it may seem to you. When you act out of love, you are loving me as you are. Do you know that? When doubts or suffering come your way, remember me and call on me. I will be with you and will give you strength. Above all, when temptation comes your way, then cry out, cry out with trust and determination. I am with you, and I will answer. Then we are both loving one another as we are.

(author unknown)

When we let our hearts be touched and moved by prayers like these, it is important to pause and glorify and thank God for what He is doing for us through His Spirit. When, in addition, we let the sentiments that moved us lead us to changing our attitudes and behaviour, then *we are letting Christ live within us.* Thus, we are letting Christ continue His Incarnation in our lives today. This is a great mystery of God's love for us.

I give you here a prayer that a friend who is very close to God advised me about. He told me that, in his own prayer, God had told him that He wished to give me a prayer – not for myself but for His people – when I was ready to receive it.

I had been very sceptical about such 'messages' but I was proved wrong on all occasions. It is wise and necessary to 'test the various spirits' and discern the presence of the Holy Spirit, but *our motivation* has also to be tested! Sometimes we are sceptical just to make sure that *we* are not going to be fooled; at other times, we like our reputation for sanity and sound 'middle-of-the-road' spirituality to be untarnished. We can run the risk, through this approach, of missing Jesus in our life as we continue our journey!

Early on a Sunday morning about a month later, I wakened . . . I grabbed pencil and paper, as the prayer was rising up within me. All I had to do was write it out properly. This prayer, *'Lord when will I learn?'*, according to reports has helped many people. One elderly man, who had lost all his property and was near-penniless, learnt that he was drawn to pray this slowly as his thanksgiving after Holy Communion. He was able to be real and to talk to God about his anger . . . eventually that was healed and love developed. The lines in bold type are places where, as it was pouring out of me, I recognised that these were personal to myself – and precious. Later, I asked God about this. I wanted to know if I had, somehow, misheard Him. He made it very clear that what He gives to one is for all His people if it helps them.

Lord, I rejoice to come before You
naked, with no defences
before Love, who is God.
I seek You alone,
not even Your gifts
great though they are,
You alone, my God.

Only in the light of Your presence
held in Your love
dare I let Your light
reveal my darkness.
Strangely – in the light of Your love
I can bear – indeed be glad
to be stripped of the false need
to appear whole even before You
who know the truth of me!

You look on my fragility,
my humanity,
my need to be active
over-busy about many things

seen to be achieving
seen to be working for You
earning Your approval!

O God who is Love
how can You bear it.
You traffic only in love,
in an open heart
not in merit or earnings.
You do not need spiritual savings
stored up against a rainy day
When will I learn?

You seek a heart that trusts and loves,
believes, surrenders and
knows it has nothing of itself,
standing in need of nothing
but genuine love.
When will I learn
that though I make my heart a den of thieves
of sordid traffic
You Father, Son and Spirit
still live even within me?

When will I learn
that Your delight is to be with me
healing bondage to all darkness
moving obstacles to love,
releasing from blindness,
self-righteousness,
self-sufficiency?

You want to make my heart Your home.

GOD'S DELIGHT

You want to see the inn of my heart
always open, ready to receive,
'Welcome home, Jesus my Love'.
Whether You come weary, broken
in neighbour, stranger, searcher,
a burden or gift
joy or sorrow
alone or with Your body
carrying a cross to be shared
or a Resurrection grace,
always
at every step of the way
You look to see
my heart open wide
'Welcome home, Jesus my Love'.
When will I learn
how my welcome warms You?

Home is where we are at ease
sure of a welcome
where we belong
have a right to be
a right to come as we are
a right to find warmth and love.
Jesus, my heart is Your home.
You gave me all I am and have
You gave me my heart as our home
without You I am and have nothing
with You I am and have love.
Love – the one thing necessary
the universal longing, needing
no explanation nor clarification –
the sisterhood and brotherhood

of all Your people.

Love – a crumb or a banquet
a goldmine or a cup of water.
Love is God,
in Him
is oneness with people
and with all creation.
No inns closed to Your birth
no lodging to hardness of heart
Love is home.
Come home and in the heart
be with God and His people.

In the depths of a heart
His tenderness can say:
'Let My love well up within you
overflowing barren deserts
bringing unheard of fruitfulness.'
Your love – abundant harvest
Your love – light of the world
scattering the dark, the wayward,
transforming the blindness of 'me alone'
bringing Light that is 'God Alone'.

Light that is Jesus
Spirit that is Love,
lead us home
to rest in the Father's arms
holding all in being,
safe secure.
Your kingdom comes in the fruit of light –
peace and faith

trust and hope
joy and love.

O Jesus, when will I learn?
Help us all to learn
help us to come home
where the Father and You breathe in the Spirit
'Welcome home, child whom We love.'

Another prayer written by G. Nintemann OP, is a favourite with many. It is called *'Persons are Gift'*. If we reflect on this with an open mind and heart, we can rediscover our own value in the eyes of Christ. Out of the acceptance of our own worth, we are better able to look at and own our attitude to other people. We can find ourselves confronted and perhaps recall the words of Christ: 'Whatever you do to one of these my least brethren, you do to me' (Matt. 25: 40).

Persons are gift . . .
at least Jesus thought so: 'Father, I want those you have given to me to be where I am.'

Persons are gifts which the Father sends me wrapped.
Some are wrapped beautifully;
They are very attractive when I first see them.
Some come in ordinary wrapping paper.
Others have been mishandled in the mail.
Once in a while there is a 'Special Delivery',
Some persons are gifts which are loosely wrapped;
Others very tightly.
But the wrapping is not the gift.
It is so easy to make this mistake.

PRAYER

Sometimes the gift is very easy to open,
Sometimes I need others to help.
Is it because they are afraid?
Does it hurt?

Maybe they have been opened up before and thrown away.
Could it be that the gift is not for me?

I am a person,
therefore I am a gift, too.
A gift to myself, first of all,
the Father gave myself to me.
Have I ever really looked inside the wrappings?
Afraid to?
Perhaps I have never accepted the gift that I am . . .
Could it be that there is more inside the wrappings
than I think there is?
Maybe I've never seen the wonderful gift that I am.
Could the Father's gifts be anything but beautiful?
I love the gifts which those who love me give me;
Why not this gift from the Father?

And I am a gift to other persons.
And I willing to be given by the Father to others?
A person for others?
Do others have to be content with the wrappings . . .
never permitted to enjoy the gift?

Every meeting of persons is an exchange of gifts.
But a gift without a giver is not a gift;
it is a thing, devoid of relationship to a giver or givee.
Friendship is a relationship between persons
who see themselves as they truly are;

gifts of the Father to each other, for others . . .
brothers, sisters.
A friend is a gift not just to me
but to others through me.
When I keep my friend and possess him, I destroy his 'giftedness'.
If I save his life for me, I lose it;
If I lose it for others, I save it.

Persons are gifts, received and given, like the Son.
Friendship is the response of person-gifts to the Father-giver.
Friendship is Eucharist.

'Just a whisper, Lord' brings us back to the theme of an earlier chapter in this book, when love and delight became one.

Just a whisper, Lord!

Lord, You are God
God is Love.

To love
is to give not counting the cost

God's Delight
is both to love and be loved.

In loving, God's Delight
is to embrace each one:
the weakest, the not so weak,
to protect yet empower!

PRAYER

In being loved, God's Delight
is the Father's glory
in the Spirit's love
through the Son's empowering
their child's free response.

God's Delight
is sharing the story
– child to child –
of the wonder of God
alive within us
pouring His life into
our words, our actions,
that in His dying
we may live!

O God, our God,
how great You are
yet humble and small,
tiny in Your crib
hidden in Your world
waiting to be found
delighting, though God,
to play hide and seek
with Your beloved children!

Stanza six brings alive again the concept of Christ alive within us, living His Incarnation in us!

the wonder of God
alive within us
pouring His life into
our words, our actions,

that in His dying
we may live!

There is a childlikeness and yet a poignancy in the last verse when this tiny infant – yet God – is *delighting to play hide and seek with us.* When God plays hide and seek with us, He is attracting us into spiritual depths through the joy of our humanity, the joy of letting His Incarnation live in us today. He is truly hidden in every part of His world, especially in little things, even in darkness. Eagerly He awaits our finding Him through the Spirit; His delight spills over into our humanity, His joy mingles with ours.

It is by our staying with Jesus, in verses like this, that we are prepared for the deeper spirituality which is offered in the desert and desert prayer, our theme in the next chapter.

The advantage of using prayers like these which are emotive is that unconsciously we move from vocal prayer, which remains so often prayer of the *mind*, to prayer of the *heart*. It becomes a very good mix and we can gently move from the mind to the feelings and let ourselves become more involved; then again, we can give the mind the freedom to apply what has moved us to our daily living, our ordinary relationships, and discern what changes must be made if we are to obey the command of the Lord: 'Love one another as I have loved you' (John 15:12).

The 'cenacle experience'

Before I move to the special kind of prayer which I associate with the desert experience, I would like to draw your attention to what I call a 'cenacle experience'.

This is a simple form of prayer which can immerse you in God for a few precious moments throughout your day. I build it on the Gospel experience and on Acts 1:4–5.

Christ told his disciples to await the *coming of the Spirit*. They were to be witnesses of the death and resurrection of Christ, and were to preach repentance and forgiveness of sins in His name. To do this, they needed to be *'clothed with power from on high'* (Luke 24: 46–9). And so He gave them the command, 'Do not leave Jerusalem, but wait for the gift my Father promised, which you have heard me speak about. For John baptised with water, but in a few days, *you will be baptised with the Holy Spirit'* (Acts 1: 4–5). As we cannot even say 'Abba Father' without the Holy Spirit, we recognise that we need to implore God frequently *to cover us with the Holy Spirit, to fill us and mould us*. This is the purpose of the cenacle experience.

> *We pause* – while typing, cooking, before making an important business call, or whatever; we become physically still; we focus on Jesus who is within us, waiting to pour out His Spirit upon us, delighting the Father.

> *We entrust ourselves* in silence and stillness to God – having no plans, no words, nothing of ourselves, longing to be totally dependent on God, waiting for the gift of His love, which is the Spirit.

To write or to read this and to understand takes time; *with practice*, one can be filled with quiet and abandonment in a few moments. With God all things are possible.

The cenacle experience prepares us for the prayer of the desert. It is all God's gift. It is not for special people

– unless you call little people (those who have trust in God, who hand over all to Him while they wait and listen and obey) 'special people'. I do! It is a very rewarding prayer-experience and glorifies God greatly. It means, however, taking seriously the self-emptying process which prepares us for the birthing of Christ within us by leaving space for the over-shadowing of our whole being by the Holy Spirit.

These are just a few prayers that have been effective and healing for some people. Use what suits you and leads you to be at ease with prayer of quiet, or prayer of the heart.[2] If the desert experience is for you, God will lead you there in His time.

A Chance to Reflect

Be still and know that I am God
(Ps. 46:10)

When you seek me with all your heart, I will let you find me.
(Jer. 29:13–14)

You keep him in perfect trust whose mind is stayed on you
because he trusts in you. Trust in the Lord forever,
for the Lord is an everlasting rock.

And I said to you: 'Do not take fright, do not be afraid . . .
Yahweh your God goes in front of you and will be fighting
on your side . . . in the wilderness you saw . . . how
Yahweh carried you, as a man carries his child, all along
the road you travelled on the way to this place.'
(Deut. 1:29–32)

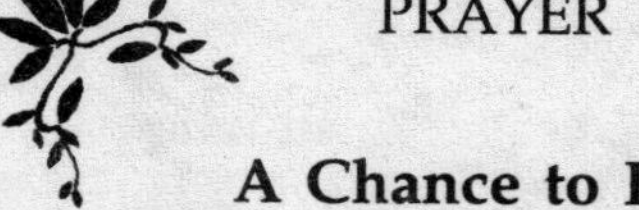

A Chance to Pray

Raise me up when I am most afraid,
I put my trust in You;
in God whose word I praise,
in God I put my trust, fearing nothing.
What can man do to me?
(Ps. 56:3–4)

Lord, draw me ever closer to You that I may grow in faith and hope and love . . .

I do love You, but I want to love You with and for all other people who need support as I so often need it. Bind us together, Lord, to glorify You.

10

THE DESERT AND PRAYER

The desert experience with its special kind of prayer is definitely not what suits everybody. God has His own way of speaking to each of us and He will ensure that – if we are eager and ready to move deeper into our spirit – we will get the nourishment that is healthy for us. For example, many of my friends benefit greatly from the 'Jesus Prayer': 'Lord Jesus Christ, Son of God, have mercy on me, a sinner.' Richard Foster in his book on prayer presents this very well.[1]

When I speak here of the 'desert experience', I have in mind just one kind of desert experience which God invited me to use. There are other forms of desert retreat. It happened that I found myself in a situation which always leaves me uneasy and uncomfortable – namely *physically isolated at night in a building far from other humans*. (It stems, I think, from infancy when the Black-and-Tans attacked our village, shooting at random. Maryanne had bathed me and was holding me, when a stray bullet skimmed our heads; lights went out and pandemonium raged. So I'm told. We children with Maryanne were sent out to the country to a 'safe' house and remained there for a few weeks. Whatever the roots of this fear, I avoid that kind of isolation at night whenever I can!)

It happened, however, that I became separated from others – despite my fears – in an area which had become unsafe. I was afraid and for three nights I could not sleep. I was badly needing sleep as the ministry in which I was involved at the time was demanding. A friend offered to change rooms with me after unwelcome voices were heard outside my window on the previous night. But I sensed that – for whatever reason – God had some plan for me which, in time, would unfold. As I was eventually going off to sleep, muttering to God about being so isolated, I heard somewhere in my being: '*Isolation can be fruitful.*' I was scheduled to address a group the following day. As I was scheduled to give talks, I completely forgot that 'word' spoken to me on the previous night. It was only when I met a few kindred spirits during the day that, to my amazement, I heard myself saying to them words that were not of my devising: 'What would you think if I were to suggest that a few of us go to a quiet, isolated place for about six days, just to be alone with God in total silence and simplicity, seeking Him alone, not His gifts, in fact coming "naked" before Him?'

That was the beginning of 'desert retreats' as I understand them. We had four such retreats in the past year and two more are arranged for this year. I find them so powerful that I feel called to continue this ministry, although I have handed over all 'Light Out of Darkness' retreats to trained leaders.

Much prayer and discernment are the instruments used to discover whom the Lord calls to participate.

When I was talking about the title of this book in Chapter 4, I said a lot about the simplicity of the format of the retreat itself. Here I would like to say more about the kind of prayer that fits with this form of desert retreat. The prayer consists in being as present to Almighty God as one can, knowing that there are no usual 'escape hatches', if one were seeking such. There is no access to release from isolation before God through scripture, or through talking things over with a guide. There is no customary reading material. We also forego the unction of the celebration of the Eucharist; or sitting contemplatively before the Blessed Sacrament unless someone experiences a discerned call to do so. **Barrenness, nakedness, nothingness are the options**! One can also risk being deceived by indulging oneself in writing up one's cherished notes. It seems unavoidable that in doing so, one's focus becomes riveted on *self* rather than on the 'nakedness' of God who emptied Himself for us. There is no space at all in such a retreat for boning up on past talks, or preparing for coming events, or in creativity of any kind. The Creator provides all.

God, God alone, is the centre of each day and each moment of the day. There is nowhere else to go. One is reminded of the wisdom of the words of Peter: 'To whom shall we go? You have the words of eternal life' (John 6:68). That is exactly what happens. Having nothing, no one else but God, He gives us our manna from heaven – as His wisdom ordains. In stillness, in silence, maybe in dryness or in darkness, perhaps in endurance and difficulty, one *waits* on God, *one waits* . . . In the four desert retreats which I have made, each has been a quite different experience from the other three. Each has had 'testing' at some stage in it; the richness of each is gradually disclosed, sometimes glimpses one day, nothing perhaps on the morrow, then through the faith-sharing of a participant, a mirror reveals light for oneself. There is no one way; most of all I have discovered that the unveiling of the richness of a discovery is a slow, gradual experience, and frequently it is one's ensuing life-experience which holds the key to release light and wisdom.

Sometimes it is here, during the faith-sharing, in the presence of the *Body of Christ* that the Spirit of Christ shines His light on one or the other – to the gracing of the whole group. The depth of the sharing – or the peaceful acceptance of a participant of the barrenness and waiting – witnesses especially to the presence and the power of God. The participants are powerless except to receive whatever God chooses for each. *The richness of this total dependence on God never leaves one.* It becomes a deep conversion experience – if one is willing to keep handing over one's life to God when the retreat is over.

This 'nakedness' before God affects one's behaviour pattern (as well as one's prayer-life) more deeply than one can imagine. This is the continuing action of the Spirit to which I previously referred when I was talking about using scripture. There I spoke about the deepening process that occurs in our understanding of the depth of God's word when we 'stay' with the word, or repeat the prayer experience. It happens all the time, whether it is a repeat of a prayer experience, or a deeper listening to God, or a keener being-aware of a movement of the Spirit within us. I sometimes think that, due to too great haste and bustle, to inadequate silence and stillness, we let go what perhaps we once had – a greater delicacy of awareness and of presence to our interior movements, the indications of the presence of the Spirit of God praying within us when we do not know how to pray (Rom. 8:26). How is one's behaviour pattern affected? It seems to me that one learns to be less in a hurry, less eager to get things finished and to be ready for the next foray; one is more content just *to be*. It goes deeper than that, however, and one gets there seemingly more smoothly and more easily.

I have frequently spoken about the importance of the present moment, of the 'Now' which is the hour of salvation (2 Cor. 6:2). I find that this change in behaviour becomes very closely allied with deeper prayer, deeper Christian attitudes which take a new turn in the Spirit, occurring in the 'Now' of the present situation. Let me give an example.

We are all familiar with the everyday experience of hurry and bustle, where each person's project assumes astronomical proportions of importance – surpassing everybody else's preferences. Just one of those days! When one becomes interiorly more accustomed to stillness, to letting go to the Spirit who is in charge, to listening to His voice, His teaching or His leading, as in the desert retreat, then one is guided more easily to step aside, to withdraw from the mêlée so as to reduce the pressure for others; but also, one finds oneself standing in the gap for the most distressed, the most harassed and frankly the most annoying. In the silence of the retreat, I became amazed at a different viewpoint that frequently emerges, unsolicited. I saw my 'jaundiced' eye – which I had actually thought had been a gentle eye, until the Spirit revealed a better vision! This has led me in ordinary daily life to try to enter more deeply into the eye of the hurricane which is howling; there I have previously learnt – and the retreat renews the teaching – that in the eye of the storm or the hurricane, the Spirit of peace and quiet resides to give wisdom to those who seek.

All of this, I'm sure, is speaking to you clearly of the thrust of this whole book: namely, our being taught by God's Spirit how to let Christ live deeply within us in the ordinary daily occurrences of life; it is thus that the Risen Christ continues His Incarnation within you, within me, and God is glorified. Not only is God *glorified*, but we know that He is *delighted* with every movement that is connected with our salvation story, our mutual love-story with Jesus Christ!

It may perhaps be beneficial if I share with you an unusual feature of the desert retreats as we experienced them. Somehow, a general message was received for *the Body of Christ*, in a different way, each time. The emphasis, however, was always on the whole Body, even when an individual was the recipient.

First words

During the first retreat, I found that I was too concerned about the flow of it and too anxious lest we got it wrong. What a mistake in my focus! In a near-despondent mood, I was just sitting there when words came to me. I heard them but as if in a haze or darkly. I thought I might be hallucinating. It was – as usual – only later and even now, much later, that I experience their power. They are in that prayer 'Lord, when will I learn?' that is in the preceding section on Prayer with a Difference. In the third last stanza comes:

Let My love well up within you
overflowing barren deserts

bringing unheard of fruitfulness.

I can only witness to the effects of those lines on my life. They only seem to come to mind when the going is rough, or when I need a clear reminder of God's love and His power. Then, when I become still, and say those lines slowly, filled with trust, all I can say is that doubt, darkness, apathy, whatever, melts, and the power of His love brings life to my barren desert, and the effect is peace.

The measure of my need to receive those words originally is the following fact. When I heard them and accepted them during the desert retreat, my first thought – to my shame – was for others, for those barren deserts who didn't know God! Very soon, God disabused my mind of this folly. *I myself am the barren desert* which the Spirit of Love, the Holy Spirit of God, has to keep alive, and fruitful so as to be able to be used by Almighty God. This is true of *all* of us, no matter how close we seem to be to God. We are all barren deserts without God. It is His love which irrigates us, and brings our wilderness to new life! This is the message that applies to the whole Body, as I said above, even when an individual was the original recipient.

Second retreat with a second message

This particular retreat was slow getting off the ground. There were various reasons for that. Yet God got through to us in the end, in His own way at His own pace. Here was a case where God spoke through the whole Body, not through an individual. He gave a clear call to love, seeking not intellectuals but *lovers* – that is, people who would love the Lord their God and love

God's people. This message came to an all-Irish group and applied specifically to the Irish situation, but the group recognised it had worldwide implications for them as well.

This message spurred us on. With this group, the message of the Incarnation had taken root and had been confirmed by others outside our retreat group, who did not know what we were about. We sincerely desired that, as a group, we would give birth to Christ and to His love, as *our* experience of Incarnation. We committed ourselves to giving priority to love of God and love of our neighbour. We agreed that each day, at either 12.00 midday or 6.00 p.m., we would say the Angelus Prayer[2] 'to commemorate the greatest love there ever was, the love which expressed itself in the Incarnation of Christ'. Before we left the retreat, a message was delivered to us from a group that had prayed for us. They told us – without knowing anything of our thoughts, or plans – 'Each day, we prayed for you at 12.00 by saying the Angelus to commemorate the Incarnation'! What more consoling message could we have received from God that Emmanuel was truly with us!

Third retreat

In Chapter 4, on the title of this book, I have already told you the story of how I heard the words that Christ spoke to me: 'This is God's delight.' In answer to my query, 'Why all this?', He answered: 'Because you have let God use you to bring His people to Him.'

Having seen the picture of Christ embracing His people, the Body of Christ, I asked: 'How can we celebrate? We have no paten.' And His answer of delight: 'What is wrong with My heart?' The result of that is that this book,

I hope, will increase God's delight by our coming daily closer to God, our Saviour. We will also greatly delight Him by spreading the Good News of His love and care for each one of us, and we celebrate His coming by letting Christian joy fill us to overflowing. This message, which I received, is applied to the whole Body of Christ, especially when we surrender ourselves to Him, letting Him use us for others. This may be through kindness of heart, through encouraging words or actions; in short when we put the well-being of others first.

Fourth retreat

I was aware of the deep humility of an elderly Jesuit priest of eighty-two years who was one of our participants in this retreat. In the United States, he had the reputation of being a prophet, but in our group, he was unassuming, wrapped in God.

The retreat went very well and I thought we had nearly come to the end point! On the very last evening, however, we received a message from a Sister who had been unavoidably prevented from joining us by deaths in her community. She had stayed with us in prayer, however, and now sent us the following message which she herself had received in prayer for herself but also for us. I admit that, at first, I was a little annoyed at its 'untimeliness', as I thought. (As if God can ever be untimely!) The humility and wisdom of our elderly Jesuit priest, however, set me on the right track. He read the message carefully – which I had scarcely done – and then said: 'This is pure gold.' When we all took it, reflected on it and prayed, we too found the gold nugget which has helped us and drawn us since our receiving it. This is how it reads:

During your time of silence, be still, not agitated and let Me work in and through you. In these days of solitude, I will help you strip down layers and layers of self-centredness in thought and habit, of which you are unaware. If you remain wrapped in layers of self-concern, you cannot step into the adventures I have prepared for you. Be willing. Centre on Me only – this will fan the flame of your faith in Me. Think only of the 'Now' – the rest is futile. Praise our Father for the glory of each moment when you live it with Me, and thank the Father for the joy of being alive.

Once again, we are reminded of our innate frailty but that God's love draws good out of all things. I have been greatly enlightened by becoming now much more aware of self-centredness in thought and habit, of which one can be quite unaware. Here Romans 8:26–27 comes in again, by my asking the Spirit to pray for me in this unknowing and unawareness. What a weakness that is! The Spirit has responded generously by granting a greater sensitivity to the care that is necessary to exercise over one's thoughts and one's behaviour. 'Let your behaviour change according to the new mind that is in you' (Rom. 12:2). If we can eliminate darkness of thought, rash judgments, carelessness of the tongue, a lot more glory will accrue to Almighty God. If we can catch the unloving thought and hand it straight over to God, we are being of real service to God and to the world.

It is frightening how the 'unkind, ungenerous thought' can catch fire and spread. Very quickly, the thought becomes a certainty, a judgment and then a prejudice!

Soon the 'fire' can become a conflagration, when the tongue takes hold of the poisoned thought and 'all hell is let loose'. If our 'heart' is kind and gentle, taught by Christ: 'Learn of me; for I am gentle and lowly of heart' (Matt. 11:29), then the thoughts that flow from such a heart will bring peace, flowing like a river. If this became the way of life of the Body of Christ – as God so desires – then, indeed, true peace, lasting peace, the peace that is the presence of Christ living among us will be realised. Let us pray for that gift individually, and as members of His Body.

A Chance to Reflect

Contemplation is nothing else than
a secret and peaceful and loving inflow of God.

St John of the Cross

One word spake the Father
which Word was His Son
and this Word he speaks ever
in eternal silence
and in silence
must it be heard
by the soul.

St John of the Cross

LOVE ALONE
attracts me . . .
I leave myself entirely in His Hands.
He is my God
and I need
no other compass.
St Therese of the Child Jesus

LOVE
was
our Lord's Meaning.
Julian of Norwich

When evening comes, you will be examined in love.
St John of the Cross

A Chance to Pray

'Everything passes! In the evening of life
Love alone remains.'
Elisabeth of the Trinity

Lord, Beloved,
teach me how to go out of myself, to forget myself,
so that I may learn to cling to You alone
and in doing so to become one with every sister and brother
so that I may love them as You have loved us.
Amen.

Jesus, time is passing and so is the golden
opportunity to know You better, to begin my
heaven here on earth by resting in You, by

bringing others to know You and to stay close to You, as other people have helped me.

When I pray for myself, Jesus, let me always include other people who have nobody to pray for them or with them. Your heart longs for all Your children and today is my golden chance of trying to bring those who are lost or hurt or angry close to You.

All for You, dear Jesus, all for You, Amen.

11

MARY, THE MOTHER OF JESUS AND OUR MOTHER

I hope that in our journey together so far, we have become more aware of God's delight in us, His children, becoming more 'at home' with our Saviour who has journeyed far to make His home with us to save us.

In the preparation and writing of this book, I have been keenly aware of God's longing to come closer to us, His people. I have felt the Father's great longing that we will allow ourselves to be touched by the power of God and open up to receive generously His chosen one, His delight 'who came unto his own and his own received him not' (John 1:11).

With increasing clarity, I have been made aware that the mystery of the Incarnation is essentially an experience of 'togetherness', of a coming together, a continual movement into unity, harmony, oneness:

- the Word Eternal in becoming 'flesh' is the experience of divinity and humanity becoming one.
- the Trinity, Three in One, is fully involved: the Holy Spirit overshadows the maiden, the Word Eternal

becomes flesh and the will of the Father is fulfilled and glorified.
- the Risen Christ lives within us, redeemed sinners, continuing His Incarnation, drawing us more into the image of God created by the Father, so that we 'become one, Father, just as you are in me and I am in you' (John 17:21).

And indispensable to all of this experience of salvation – the eternal plan, the action of the Spirit, the coming of the Saviour – is Mary, chosen by God to be the Mother of Jesus Christ.[1]

Not only is she the Mother of Jesus the Saviour, but from the Cross of Salvation, Jesus has given her *to us* as our Mother too. Another coming together! In this gift to us of His Mother, Jesus is saying something special if we are willing to hear. In His earthly sojourn, He needed her – as a child in the womb, as a young boy growing up, as a dreamer of God's dreams, as a lover of God's people, as one rejected by His own, as a Saviour giving all receiving little; **He** needed to be loved, encouraged, energised by sharing the same Spirit. The one dear to the Father's heart, chosen by God as His Mother to provide what was possible, was Mary. He needed her caring as did His disciples and as we do too. The children are not above the Master! Even though the Twelve knew Jesus personally, they learnt from Mary, from her example. Her love of Jesus and of them was non-possessive. She gave all, looking only to serve. Surely in the cenacle, as they waited with her for the promised coming of the Holy Spirit, her presence must have been comforting and strengthening.

I find it strengthening, for example, when I am leading

a retreat, writing a book or being sorely perplexed, to enlist the supportive prayer of others on my behalf. They do not come *between* me and God, I must take my own responsibility, but God is praised by more prayer and union of heart.

I was strongly moved by the Spirit to dedicate this book to Mary. I hesitated, avoided doing it, aware of prejudices that can exist. I sincerely regret any behaviour patterns that open the way to misunderstanding the true role of Mary. Scripture presents to us a humble, obedient, committed child of God, who today, as two thousand years ago, continuously points the way to her Son: 'Do whatever he tells you' (John 2:5). She supports every move we make towards Jesus. She does not come *between* us.

Eventually, after more prayer and when I found it difficult, indeed practically impossible, to get into the material of the book as I desired, I finally obeyed the call of Jesus. I dedicated the book to the Mother of Jesus and our Mother, and in the peace of mind that followed, I wrote from my heart, and was taught much in the writing!

I present Mary as I have come to know her in prayer, reflection, and as an influence in my life. As a good Mother values the uniqueness of each of her children and deals accordingly with them, so does Mary. My hope is that those who feel called will allow the Holy Spirit to guide them in their reflections on the Mother beloved by Jesus, thus enriching their own experience.

Mary was a woman of great faith and trust in God. I believe that Mary knew the identity of her Son from the beginning. Therefore, she knew this before the child knew. God's care of them, through dreams and messages, was reassuring, as was Elizabeth's greeting:

> Blessed are you among women, and blessed is the child you will bear! But why am I so favoured, that the Mother of my Lord should come to me? As soon as the sound of your greeting reached my ears, the baby in my womb leaped for joy. Blessed is she who has believed that what the Lord has said to her will be accomplished. (Luke 1:42–45).

Mary's beautiful response in the Magnificat – so reminiscent of Hannah's song – reveals again the same spirit which was clear at the Annunciation: *humility* as the sound basis of this wonderful event, which is the will of her God and the action of God.

Did Mary, in humility, await the action of the Holy Spirit who was leading her and was within her with regard to the identity of Jesus? It is quite conceivable that Mary waited for God's own action to indicate how or when Jesus was to learn His identity. It seems that whatever was happening in the home in Nazareth, the Spirit had been forming this child whose maturity so astounded the doctors in the Temple at the age of twelve. If, on the other hand, Mary had shared with the child Jesus all she knew, she would certainly have discerned every step of the way through the power of the Spirit.

As I said, I lean strongly towards the position that Mary let this child grow normally as children will; she would await a measure of maturity that could carry the question of His identity without unnecessary weight. As it was, by the time they settled in Nazareth, Mary, Joseph and Jesus had already experienced heavenly visitations, unexpected visitors soon after the birth bearing heavenly signs and wonders, a confirmatory message from devout Simeon, enlarging on the accepted mission of the Messiah and extending it to the whole world, and adding the prophecy that was personal to Mary, the Mother: '. . . a sword will pierce your own soul too' (Luke 2: 29–35). The enemies of the child had been experienced by Joseph and Mary and they had to be constantly on the alert.

Whatever the real situation was, the point I am trying to make here is that Mary, the Mother of Jesus and our Mother, was a woman who had given herself totally to Almighty God from her earliest years, whose **faith** was consonant with her **obedience and love**. Her **trust in God** did not waver, witnessed to by the Angel Gabriel and Elizabeth, nor has scripture ever indicated a weakening of that even when this valiant woman stood at the cross of her Son.

I see Mary's humility as the sure rock which supported her all through her amazing experience of mothering her God. Without her deep basic attitude to Almighty God, without her deep awareness of His transcendence and the creature's total dependence on Him for everything, God would not have chosen her. It was not enough to be willing to become the Mother of the Son of God; she had to be able to forget herself totally so as to be truly the handmaid to the will of God at all times. She could have no other life but that of being the handmaid of God's will, whether that meant heavenly visitations, sudden departures, pursuit by enemies, not knowing ever the timing of the next upheaval – and she and Joseph were only two frail guardians of the Son of the Almighty against the powers of evil that threatened them!

This situation demanded total readiness to obey God's

word at all times, no matter what the cost, and that meant perfect humility. God alone counted. Whatever He ordained was right. God was totally trustworthy.

Even to state that is, for me at any rate, as never before, a realisation that in Mary we have an amazing gift from God . . . a sterling woman, filled with a quality of faith and hope and love that we can admire, be grateful for, and try to esteem highly so as to follow her example. It is true that she was conceived sinless, because the vessel that was to hold the Son of God for nine months could not in any way have a blemish, however slight. This did not mean that Mary, like her Son, could not be tempted. She was truly human, a woman born to suffer!

Nazareth

The task that Mary and Joseph were asked to carry out in their modest dwelling was monumental. Sincere young couples, with the best intentions and desires to give their children the best upbringing they can, still find themselves facing many difficult challenges and decisions. While such parents hope that their offspring will do well in life, perhaps make a worthy contribution to society, they are not confronted with rearing a child 'destined to cause the falling and rising of many in Israel, and to be a sign that will be spoken against so that the thoughts of many will be revealed' (Luke 2:34–35). Such parents, as we mentioned, know that they will encounter problems, sickness, perhaps even early death, but Mary, the Mother, heard clearly prophesied by 'righteous and devout Simeon' the life of sorrow that was marked for her: 'A sword will pierce your own soul too.' Mary and Joseph followed the example of their own culture, where respect was paid to elders; Simeon was known as a man led and moved by the Spirit. They heeded therefore the prophecy with regard to Jesus which was telling them that people would either joyfully accept Him or totally reject Him. With Jesus, from His first appearance in the Temple as an infant, there was no neutral ground! It seems to be the way with people who are entrusted with a mission – much more so then with Jesus, the Son of God.

Jesus, Mary and Joseph returned to Nazareth when, like the upright Jews that they were, 'they had fulfilled everything required by the Law of the Lord'. 'And the child grew and became strong; he was filled with wisdom, and the grace of God was upon him' (Luke 2:39–40).

Scripture tells us that Jesus 'was filled with wisdom'. Mary, too, was full of grace, conceived sinless, who 'had found favour with God' (Luke 1:30). This favour would not mean an easy life nor avoidance of pain, anguish, sorrow; it brought her what obedience always brings – peace of mind and heart, despite the burdens and problems that arise. Mary's being 'filled with the Spirit' required from her continual discernment, of what was happening at that time in her home, what involvement of neighbours, of relatives, revealed of God's will or revealed of the darker side of life. **Discernment** would have been a crucial factor in Mary's decision-making, as 'being filled with the Holy Spirit' did not automatically guarantee that she was hearing God correctly. Always she remembered her humanity, her obedience to God's will, what humility demanded; always Mary would ponder, reflect and learn; always she would give first praise, glory and thanks to her God. In other words, Mary prayed continuously – understanding prayer as continuous communication with Almighty God. As a result of her prayer, her obedience, her humility, Mary's **faith** and **hope** and **love** kept increasing.

Mary, as likewise her friends Joseph, Zachary, Elizabeth and the devout Simeon, probably all shared in the spiritual tradition of the 'anawim'. This attitude of 'the little ones' is evident in Mary's *Magnificat*, Zachary's *Benedictus*, and Simeon's *prophecy*. This particular tradition of spirituality was based on Isaiah, with special emphasis on the 'suffering servant'. Jesus was probably brought up in this same tradition.

Again I ponder on this amazing woman – our Mother and the Mother of Jesus. I realise how much more 'flesh and blood' this reflection is putting on Mary for me. It is so deceptively easy to see her as the Mother of Jesus and thus take it for granted that Almighty God will take care of her for His Son's sake! This is to deny all that we ourselves know about the way grace operates and how we are all called to be responsible for the quality of our day-to-day response! Nobody knew this better than Mary, who saw at first hand how her Son Jesus devoted every breath to the quality of life that was His each day. He made choices, as we do; He discerned what God hoped for through His humanity that day, as we are called to do; He knew how other people are affected positively or adversely by our response to life and to one another – so must we; and Mary gave us, her children, the lead.

In Nazareth, therefore, Mary would teach her child to the best of her ability; likewise He would be reared and trained as befits any child of God, and this child would not in any way miss out on anything. Jesus therefore would be taught about the great love of Yahweh for His people; He would open His eyes and heart in wonder – to the delight of His parents – as the story of Israel unfolded. His keen mind grew accustomed to asking questions, to querying with unusually keen insights, as He was led by the Spirit. No wonder He made an impression in the Temple at twelve!

It was a normal household insofar as a family totally centred on God and the fulfilment of His will is normal. Jesus was exposed to right values, proper attitudes to other people; all the qualities like compassion, mercy, justice, truth, faith, hope, joy, and others were nourished in His home as we expect. **Wisdom** would shine forth in that household, wisdom which flowered in humility, obedience, hard work, contemplative space, beauty of creation; above all wisdom in recognising and in having compassion for the uniqueness of each person, the responsibility this laid on those who 'have', and the compassion due to those who 'have not'. And the gentle spirit that was the centre of this wisdom, opening her son's heart to these new experiences, was His Mother – and ours.

Scripture opens us to wisdom as we hear words referring to Mary's not understanding a saying, an event, and her response to this not-knowing: 'Mary treasured all these things in her heart and pondered on them!' I personally treasure the wisdom of God who, understanding our human need, gives us this beautiful cameo of our Mother and the Mother of Jesus. She comes across as so very human in her not-understanding, but this is where her humility shines like a jewel in God's heart: is she flustered, or upset, feverishly active to know and to learn? Of course, we would say if it were our situation: 'I ought to know so as to be able to fulfil my task properly!' But not Mary. Her humility and trust in God were pure gold. She enters into her inner being where the Spirit of God abides and there she rests and ponders. In God's time, she will be taught and He will guide her in the next step of the journey. That is her faith-stance; we can happily learn from her. She is our Mother as well as the Mother of Jesus.

Scripture

Mary was travelling to Bethlehem, ostensibly to obey the decree of the Roman Governor that a census should be taken of the entire Roman world, yet this arrogant decree worked towards the fulfilment of scripture. The town in which Joseph and his wife, Mary, had to register, since they were of the House of David, was Bethlehem. The Old Testament is filled with prophecies that the Messiah would be born in David's royal line (Isa. 11:1 4:2; Ezek. 37:24; Hos. 3:5). Mary, a true Jewish maiden, was familiar with the prophecy of Micah, who accurately predicted Christ's birthplace hundreds of years before Jesus was actually born:

> But you, Bethlehem Ephrathah,
> though you are small among the clans of Judah,
> out of you will come for me
> one who will be ruler over Israel,
> whose origins are from of old,
> from ancient times . . .
> He will stand and shepherd his flock
> in the strength of the Lord,
> in the majesty of the name of the Lord his God.
> And they will live securely, for then his greatness
> will reach to the ends of the earth.

> *And he will be their peace.* (Mic.5: 2–5 italics mine)

Christ's first coming, therefore, was heralded by the prospect of peace, as Micah says. The heavenly host which announced the birth of this child to the shepherds praised God saying:

> Glory to God in the highest,
> and on earth, peace to men on whom his favour rests. (Luke 2:14)

During His last discourses with the disciples, Jesus seems preoccupied with the theme of peace, as well as of love:

> Peace I leave with you; my peace I give you. I do not give to you as the world gives. Do not let your hearts be troubled and do not be afraid. (John 14:27)

Towards the end of the discourse, having spoken to them of the Holy Spirit and the Father's love for them, he added: 'I have told you these things, so that *in me you may have peace. In this world you will have trouble.* But take heart! I have overcome the world' (John 16:33 italics mine).

At Christ's second coming, all wars and weapons will be destroyed. Micah, the prophet, speaks now of the last days, when God will reign over His perfect kingdom:

> He will judge between many peoples
> and will settle disputes for strong nations far and wide.
> They will beat their swords into ploughshares

and their spears into pruning hooks.
Nation will not take up sword against nation,
nor will they train for war any more.
Every man will sit under his own vine
and under his own fig-tree,
and no-one will make them afraid,
for the Lord Almighty has spoken. (Mic. 4:3–4)

This time of the second coming cannot be pinpointed, but God has promised that it will arrive. This is the time of the remnant, of the last days, when God will reign over His perfect kingdom. It will be an era of peace and blessing, when war will be for ever ended (Isa. 2:2; Jer. 16:15; Joel 3:1ff; Zech. 14:9–11; Mal. 3:17–18; Mic. 4:1–8; Rev. 19–22).

I associate the theme of peace with Mary, interior peace, not as the world gives, as Christ had clearly stated, but a peace that *He* gives, that He leaves with us. 'Do not let your heart be troubled and do not be afraid.' Must Christ not have prepared Mary, during their many years in Nazareth, for the turbulence of the world which would overtake Him? The harassment of his infancy must surely have continued throughout his childhood – especially in Galilee – where an oppressive political system, extreme brutality, terrorism and corruption (political and religious) operated. Can we not hear Him say to her with such love, compassion and the gift of inner strengthening: 'In this world you will have trouble, but take heart! I have overcome the world'?

Christ knew what lay in the heart of people, He knew what His Passion would mean, for both of them, and He would strengthen her with the truth: Simeon's prophecy would be fulfilled to the bitter end and her heart would be pierced to a degree that, at this moment, may look as if she could not survive – but for love of Him, she would endure, and suffer every detail with Him of rejection by His own, betrayal by Peter, desertion, the dreadful scourging and stripping, the jeering and fickleness of the mob – and the Crucifixion. Mary's vision had become as broad as His own; He had taught her and, in love such as hers, she had grown willingly to be able to be with Him under His cross, in the crucifixion of His heart – the worst of all. His vision – as hers – went far beyond Calvary and death; His vision embraced all the evil of times in between – the devastation of His people, the destruction of life which He had bought so dearly – that they all may have life indeed.

And Mary stood by the cross. The years of faith stood her now in good stead, as did the love, the obedience, the total service, the learning in her own person the cost to Jesus of salvation, *including her own*. Mary knew that her favour with God had been bought at a great price – this total giving of her Son that all God's people be saved; and she was one who was saved!

Suffering

Can we ever understand the depths, the pain of Mary's suffering? Have we not all experienced, at least in some measure, the sharpness of pain, which belongs to one dearly beloved by us, and yet we are helpless to take it on ourselves for them? Each person's burden is his or her own.

Mary's love had been honed to a fine point by living with Jesus Christ, the Son of God, who is love. Of course, she loved her Son, her only son, with all the mother-love of which she is capable; but her sinlessness does not allow her to satisfy self by any form of possessiveness. Neither did she harden her heart when the years brought Him criticism, rejection: '"This is the carpenter's son surely . . . so where did the man get it all?" And they would not accept him . . . "a prophet is only despised in his own country and in his own house"' (Matt. 13:53–57). And again they scoffed: 'This man casts out devils only through Beelzebul, the prince of devils' (Matt. 12:22–32). Every criticism, every danger of attack – as at Nazareth when they wanted to hurl Him off the cliff – all pierced Mary, without demolishing her; she loved too well; she had to be with Him until the end and for as long as He wanted, or as long as she could serve Him and His people.

Scripture

One can well conceive how Mary studied the scriptures more zealously than ever from the time the Angel Gabriel had announced the plan of God to her. According as she learnt more about her Son, about His mission, before and after the Crucifixion, surely Mary reflected on, and pondered especially, Isaiah. As she looked at Jesus, for example, at the Feast of Cana, seeing the strength and the beauty of Him, what did such passages from Isaiah do to her?

> Here is my servant, whom I uphold,
> my chosen one in whom I delight;
> I will put my Spirit on him
> and he will bring justice to the nations.
> He will not shout or cry out,
> or raise his voice in the streets.

A bruised reed he will not break,
and a smouldering wick he will not snuff out.
(Isa. 42:1–3)

We can read those verses at a long distance, but Mary, His Mother, looking at Him, knew at first hand this gentleness in Him, and His caring for the weak and the lowly – and knew also that His enemies wanted to bring Him low. It is this quality in Mary that leaves me breathless: her ability to face the worst and yet to remain strong and calm, though so vulnerable. Again, I see it as the measure of *her faith, her trust in God, her wholehearted loving and the effect of living with Jesus.*

I find it a most disturbing yet cleansing experience to read – as Mary must have read – Isaiah, alternating between songs of hope and joy and following up with the servant songs . . . and this was her Son, who has just come in from the workshop, or down from the mountain-top, or has arrived with the disciples at Cana:

Shout for joy, O heavens;
rejoice, O earth;
burst into song, O mountains!
For the Lord comforts his people
and will have compassion on his afflicted ones.
(Isa. 49:13)

The suffering and glory of the servant:

See, my servant will act wisely;
he will be raised and lifted up and highly exalted.
Just as there were many who were appalled at him –

his appearance was so disfigured beyond that of
any man
and his form marred beyond human likeness . . .
(Isa. 52:13–14)

'Who has believed our message
and to whom has the arm of the Lord been revealed?
He grew up before him like a tender shoot,
and like a root out of dry ground.
He had no beauty or majesty to attract us to him,
nothing in his appearance that we should desire him.
He was despised and rejected by men,
a man of sorrows, and familiar with suffering,
Like one from whom men hide their faces
he was despised and we esteemed him not.
(Isa. 53:1–3)

If Mary recalled at that moment the beauty of the baby that He was, and read:

Can a mother forget the baby at her breast
and have no compassion on the child she has borne?
Though she may forget,
I will not forget you!
See, I have engraved you on the palms on my
hands. (Isa. 49:15–16)

How did she maintain her faith, her hope and her love? The only answer I know is: **'With God, nothing is impossible.'**

Let us put things into perspective: Mary is a creature, the work of Almighty God's hands, who favoured her as a daughter and chose her as the Bride of the Holy Spirit and the Mother of His Son, Jesus Christ.

Born of good Jewish parents, Joachim and Anne, she was found worthy by God to experience the visitation of the Angel Gabriel, the bearer of astounding news, as a young girl of about sixteen. We have seen the qualities that she then possessed, due to the influence of her parents, the favour of God and her own efforts to respond with all her mind and heart and spirit. Even at sixteen, she was a woman of great faith, obedience, humility and love. Her life experience, with its trauma and its gift-experience of carrying and living with Life itself, Jesus Christ, transformed her into a tower of strength, indomitable where pain, endurance, self-sacrifice and love that costs were concerned. In her own way, and in the measure that God willed for her, she bore her specific cross from that time to the end of her life.

Mary, our Mother, has much to teach us about the way to follow Jesus Christ. There was joy in her life, but the shadow of the cross was never far distant, nor can it ever be in a truly Christian life. The joy that flows into our lives from the cross is of a different order from ordinary human joy. Human joy, like the birth of a beautiful baby, is a rich and special gift, but, at its root, *the impermanence of life* itself tinges that very joy with the pain of fragility. Human joy, which is rooted in material things or transient pleasures, is ephemeral at best. The cross, or its shadow, has in it a strength like an invisible bar of gold which seems to give us a permanence of endurance, or a quality of wisdom and love which lasts and transforms all it touches into the very likeness of Christ Himself.

Nor is Mary's work for God finished with her death, because her love still continues – for her Son and therefore for His people. It is understandable that her heart aches for the folly of the world and for our blindness. If God chose to speak in Old Testament times to and through His servants, there is no special surprise in His choosing to speak through Mary, the Mother of His Son, in the secret places of our heart.

Wisdom has to be shown here, of course. There is always room for more wisdom than we, frail sinners, are renowned for on all occasions!

Wisdom also needs to be used in our devotions; exaggerations on the part of some have tended to give both to the Holy Spirit and the Blessed Mother a poor press. The sadness of that is lamentable; however, our prejudices on the other hand also need to be discerned and kept in check. Jesus Christ assures us that 'the truth sets free'. I find that any attitude of mine or of others that is too strong, is not truly open to being changed, or can arouse reactions that are far from the peace of Christ, is a prejudice. That indicates an absence of genuine loving and openness. There is need there to open and let the King of Glory enter in!

My personal relationship with Mary, my Mother

I find that personal witness to a relationship, or an event, carries a special mark of authenticity. I would like, therefore, to say where Mary, the Mother of Jesus, stands in my own life.

I have been blessed in having my own mother as a warm, loving and also challenging person to start me off in life. I owe more to her than I could ever adequately share. Maryanne, whom I mentioned in Chapter 7, never challenged me; she led me by her example to see the beauty of an open, childlike heart and attitude to life. Both of these 'mothers' surrounded me with a love that ensured security.

Both of these, also, were instrumental in different ways in introducing me to my Mother, Mary, the Mother of Jesus. Both managed, quite naturally, to communicate a warmth that was related to the Mother of God. Moreover, it helped them that I was born on the Feast of Our Lady of Lourdes. This meant that I first associated Mary with the joys of a birthday – my birthday! The birthday association also meant that Christmas to me was the celebration of the birthday of Mary's child, Jesus. That again made the relationship warm and 'family-like'. I became a Religious Sister on Mary's birthday, September 8th, as that was a customary day for such an event. All of this was the setting for me to become accustomed to relating to Mary as a Mother who seemed to take as much care of me, in a different way, as my natural mother and Maryanne. The practical effect of that in my life was that I saw Jesus as the heart and centre of Mary's life – since she was His Mother. Again, it was normal for me to recognise that Mary was 'there', but Jesus was the important one and always His interests came first. Whenever I was behaving in life as seemed fitting for a Christian, this is how it was: Jesus always centre, Mary just vaguely a reality but not encroaching in any way. Gradually, I discovered, as I grew older and hopefully more mature, that in times of trouble, especially when I didn't seem to get help or guidance from others, I became much more aware of Mary's presence in my life. I will illustrate this from a story already quoted elsewhere.[2] I felt on a certain occasion that I was caught between two pillars of authority and I had no redress. I was accustomed at this stage of my life to carry all my troubles to Jesus in the Blessed Sacrament. I used to pour out all my woes, and learnt to wait and to listen, no matter how long it took. His answer usually came in my experiencing peace and a sense of His presence. On this occasion, it seemed to my horror that Jesus was not listening. I got angry and repeated my story. Still no answer! I had nowhere else to turn to and so fear of what would happen to me increased my anger. I said out loud: 'If that's how You want it, all right. I'm going' – but in my turning around to leave the church, my eye fell on Mary, His Mother.

I, of course, didn't *want* to leave; I needed help, so I went over to her and in anguish said: 'Do you know what your Son has done to me this day? In case you don't, I'm going to tell you.' Which I did. Psychologically, I now understand, it helped me to pour out my story – in all, three times, twice to her Son and once to her – and so I became quiet and was in a listening frame of mind. Then I heard, in my heart, an answer that influenced the rest of my life: *'You can get bitter and you will wither and everything and everyone you touch will wither; or,* **you can trust my Son,** *and you will grow and everything and everyone you touch will grow.'* I was left to reflect and decide. But my heart was singing. I walked out of that church floating on air. I just wasn't fully down to earth. As I walked through long corridors, I became aware that 'someone' passed me, but I really was still floating. Then I heard a voice: 'Sister, you are smiling. How can you?' I looked at her – one of the authority pillars referred to earlier – and knew, to my amazement, that no trace of bitterness remained in my heart for her; I just felt

I wanted to share something of what I had received from Jesus through Mary, my Mother. I said: 'Yes, I have discovered today that God is really in His heaven and His heaven is my heart.'

Ever since that, I am aware that while I can get angry or hurt, I have never been tempted to become bitter. Moreover, Mary and I entered into a new relationship, though I only gradually became aware of it. Now, whenever Mary's Son is about to offer me a new challenge or to ask me for something really difficult, I become faintly aware first of Mary's presence. She is more in my mind and in my heart – just that. I'm not really fully aware of her until I find myself actually in the middle of something that is too big for me. My heart is willing to do as God wants, but my strength does not match up. Then, somehow, I become calm, more surrendered, more aware that Jesus said: 'My grace is sufficient for you.' I become more aware of the Blessed Trinity and that Mary is near. It may take a long time for me to surrender and do what He wants, but I feel supported and loved.

My experience of Mary, my Mother and the Mother of Jesus, is that she is *always* the handmaid of the Lord. She is always labouring – in whatever way that is done in heaven – to help us, her children, to bring Him to new birth in our lives. She still suffers with Him in His suffering for us and she longs for us to become 'little children', for such is the kingdom of heaven.

Whatever honour is paid to Mary, it is honour paid to her God who made her in His image. Mary always keeps pointing the way to her Son. Humility – which is Truth – is her precious jewel: to His glory.

Mary, our Mother is the delight of God because she

has been so closely involved with our salvation. May she continuously help us to come to know Jesus Christ, in and through the power of the Spirit to the glory of the Eternal Father.

A Chance to Reflect

My Soul glorifies the Lord,
My Spirit rejoices in God my Saviour.
For He has blessed me lavishly,
and makes me ready to respond.
He shatters my little world
and lets me be poor before Him.
He takes from me all my plans
and gives me more than I can hope for or ask.
He gives me opportunities, and the ability
to become free, and burst through my boundaries.
He gives the strength to be daring,
to build on Him alone, for He shows Himself as
the ever greater one in my life.
He has made known to me this:
IT IS IN MY BEING SERVANT
THAT IT BECOMES POSSIBLE
FOR GOD'S KINGDOM
TO BREAK THROUGH
HERE AND NOW.
(English translation from German by Olga Warnke IBVM)

A Chance to Pray

Dear Mary, as a child I remember hearing the story that when St Peter closed the doors of heaven and would not let sinners in that you, Mother Mary, used to open the windows! Now that I'm older, I ask you, Mary, to keep praying for all of us your children, so that windows, doors and every crack in heaven may open wide.

EPILOGUE

I have great hope for the future of our believing Church.

This hope rests on our honest desire for a better world, but most especially on the power of the Incarnation.

All God needs to work the miracle of His transforming love in us, is our open and trusting heart.

My own experience – which is all anyone can offer with integrity – is that, as a result of breathing the Incarnation during the writing of this book, I have happily been led back to basics. The basics of *faith, hope and love* – truly life-giving!

In the lowliness and simplicity of ordinary, daily events, **the Risen Christ** – incarnate in the believer – **transforms the ordinary into the transparency of the Eternal.**

We, in whom these daily miracles happen, are scarcely aware of the power of the Spirit, acting on our behalf, despite our human limitations. Such is the miracle of God's work!

We are invited to contribute our 'mite' – whatever is our best effort – knowing, however, that without the love of our heart, the offering, be it a banquet, is of little use.

Let us live in faith so that when Christ returns, He will indeed find *faith* on earth.

Let us keep our focus always on Christ, the Light of the World, the hope of all nations; and our *hope* will flourish and delight God.

Let our hearts overflow with the gift of His own *love,* so that it will well up within us, bringing unheard-of-fruitfulness.

In the wonder of Your Incarnation
Your eternal Word has brought to the eyes of faith
a new and radiant vision of Your glory.
In Him we see our God made visible
and so are caught up in the love of the God we cannot see.[3]

NOTES

Chapter 3: Scripture

1 *A Way of Life* and *Light Out of Darkness* are the first two books in this trilogy; *God's Delight* is Book Three. *A Way of Life* (Veritas Publications, Dublin, 1985) has been incorporated into *Light Out of Darkness* (Hodder & Stoughton, 1993).

Chapter 8: The Holy Spirit

1 *Light Out of Darkness*, pp. 4–32; specific references to the Holy Spirit. Throughout the whole book, the presence and action of the Holy Spirit is highlighted. Video Two (see below) features a talk on the Holy Spirit.

Three videos on *Light Out of Darkness* are now available:

Video One: Useful for those who lead groups in the programmes provided in *Light Out of Darkness.*

Videos Two and Three: The talks by the author on both these videos highlight the spirituality of the programmes.

Video Two: The Incarnation; The Holy Spirit.

Video Three: The Body of Christ; Living Incarnationally Today.

Availability in England:

Books: Chris Heath, 55 Fornham Road, Bury St. Edmunds, Suffolk, IP32 6AW; Maranatha, 102 Irlam Road, Flixton, Manchester, M41 6JT.

Videos: Chris Heath as above; St. Paul's, 199 Kensington High St.,

London, W8 6BA; Veritas Bookshop, Lower Avenue, Leamington Spa, Warwickshire, CV31 3NP.
Availability in Ireland:
Books/Videos:
Fr. Dan-Joe O'Mahony, OFM. Cap., Capuchin Friary, Raheny, Dublin 5; Veritas Bookshop, Lower Abbey Street, Dublin 1; or any good Christian bookshop.

2 *Light Out of Darkness*, pp. 22–26. Discernment is used throughout all programmes of the book.

3 The 'weekend' in question was organised by the Maranatha Community, whose leader is Dennis Wrigley. This is an inter-denominational Christian Community committed to unity, renewal and healing. For fourteen years, the Community has been obedient to listening to the voice of God and obeying His word. It is Spirit-filled. This Community has been singularly blessed, is spreading fast, and has now many European connections.

Chapter 9: Prayer

1 *Light Out of Darkness*, pp. 34–43, 104–11, 170–7.

2 *Simple Prayer* by Wendy Mary Beckett (Carmelite Monastery, Quidenham, Norfolk, England) is essential reading for everyone who is sincere about prayer.

Chapter 10: The Desert and Prayer

1 Richard Foster, in his book *Prayer* (Hodder & Stoughton, 1992) p. 128, gives a lot of help on what he calls 'Breath Prayer', the most famous of which he says is the 'Jesus Prayer'.

2 The 'Angelus Prayer' recalls the mystery of the Annunciation when the Angel Gabriel visited Mary inviting her to become mother of the Lord Incarnate through the power of the Spirit. Mary's humble response was that of the handmaid of the Lord, the servant who listened eagerly and obeyed. Today, as always, Mary – Mother of God and our Mother – remains humble, loving and committed to God's will. In some places, the church bell rings at midday to remind people of this mystery, which they commemorate by saying the Angelus.

NOTES

Chapter 11: Mary, the Mother of Jesus and our Mother

1 *Light Out of Darkness*, pp. 227–30.
2 Ibid. p. 229.
3 From 'The Nativity Preface' in *The Roman Missal* (Collins, 1974) p. 406.